OXFORD BUSINESS ENGLISH SKILLS

Effective

NEGOTIATING

JEREMY COMFORT

with YORK ASSOCIATES

D0746547

OXFORD UNIVERSITY PRESS 1998

Oxford University Press,
Great Clarendon Street, Oxford OX2 6DP

Oxford New York
Athens Auckland Bangkok Bombay
Calcutta Cape Town Dar es Salaam Delhi
Florence Hong Kong Istanbul Karachi
Kuala Lumpur Madras Madrid Melbourne
Mexico City Nairobi Paris Singapore
Taipei Tokyo Toronto

and associated companies in
Berlin Ibadan

Oxford and *Oxford English*
are trade marks of Oxford University Press

ISBN 0 19 457247 1
© Oxford University Press

First published 1998

Acknowledgements

Riding the Waves of Culture, Trompenaars
Hampden-Turner, 2nd edition ©1997
Intercultural Management Publishing, the
Netherlands, is gratefully acknowledged as
the source for many of the cultural concepts
introduced in the *Culture and tactics*
sections of the units.

I would also like to thank friends and
colleagues at York Associates for their
support throughout the development of the
Oxford Business English Skills series.
I would particularly like to acknowledge the
contribution of Derek Utley. This series
would never have seen the light of day
without the pioneering and innovative work
he did on our own earlier communication
skills series.

Illustrations by: Neil Gower pp13, 14, 15;
Technical Graphics Department, OUP

Cartoons by Nigel Paige
Photography by Paul Freestone
Cover illustration by Adam Willis

**The publishers would like to thank the
following for permission to reproduce
photographs:**

The Imagebank: p40 (photographers W.
Bokelberg, Romilly Lockyer x 2, Don Klumpp)

Typeset in ITC Franklin Gothic
and Adobe Minion

Printed in Spain

Contents

Unit		Communication skills	Culture and tactics	Language knowledge	Negotiating practice
1	**Preparing the ground** page 8	agreeing objectives, strategy, and roles	task- versus person-orientation	welcome and introductions	preparation and making opening introductions
2	**Setting the agenda** page 16	structuring and controlling the negotiation process	organic versus systematic working cultures	sequencing and linking	controlling the negotiation process
3	**Establishing positions** page 24	presenting your position, getting feedback	direct versus indirect communication	asking for and giving feedback	establishing positions
4	**Clarifying positions** page 30	active listening, effective questioning	individuals versus teams	asking questions, showing interest	clarifying positions
5	**Managing conflict** page 38	avoiding personal criticism	conflict versus collaboration	downtoning your language	handling conflict
6	**Making and responding to proposals** page 46	encouraging responses, making counter-proposals	emotional versus neutral behaviour	making suggestions and proposals	making and responding to proposals
7	**Bargaining** page 52	maintaining positive communication	high-context versus low-context cultures	exerting pressure and making conditions	bargaining practice
8	**Conclusion and agreement** page 60	summarizing and agreeing follow-up	win-win versus win-lose	concluding and closing	closing the negotiation

Introduction

Introduction to the course

Negotiating is very much a key communication skill for all Business English learners. Although you may not be involved in high-level international negotiations, most of you will have to negotiate with colleagues, bosses, customers, and suppliers at some stage in your career. Negotiating effectively promises some of the biggest prizes of all communication skills – the right deal for the company, a salary rise, a budget increase, even a day off work. It is a sophisticated skill because it requires the negotiator to be competent in all key communication and language skills and to often maintain their performance under pressure. The skilled negotiator must also be aware of cultural differences which can so easily lead to communication breakdown.

Effective Negotiating is divided into eight units which approach the skills and language step by step. Starting with preparation and opening, through clarifying and dealing with conflict to bargaining and concluding, the learner is taken through a variety of practice activities which aim to develop both confidence and competence. At the same time, each unit addresses a key cultural issue which can affect the success of a negotiation.

Course components

The course consists of four components: a video, a Student's Book, an audio cassette, and a Teacher's Book.

The Video

The video, which lasts approximately 30 minutes, is the central component of the course and acts as a springboard for the all the activities in the Student's Book. Based around a negotiation between a Belgium-based multinational and a British IT company, it illustrates key moments from a typical business negotiation, both internally, and between the teams.

The Student's Book

The book consists of eight units which correspond to those in the video. Each unit is divided into four sections: *Communication skills*, *Culture and tactics*, *Language knowledge*, and *Negotiating practice*.

The *Communication skills* section identifies and practises key negotiating skills which are illustrated in the video, and aims to involve the learner in a process of feedback, evaluation, and development. The *Culture and tactics* section raises a number of key cultural issues which may lead to misunderstanding and communication breakdown, and looks at how such problems might be avoided. The *Language knowledge* section, supported by the audio cassette, focuses on and expands the learner's knowledge in key functional and lexical areas. The concluding *Negotiating practice* section gives the learner the opportunity to put communication skills, cultural awareness, and language knowledge into practice, using a variety of role-plays and simulations.

The Audio Cassette

This consists of approximately 50 minutes of extracts from a wide range of negotiations and forms the basis of the listening activities in the *Language knowledge* section of the Student's Book.

The Teacher's Book

This book provides an introduction to the course from a teacher's point of view. It is intended as a guide to help the teacher to handle the different components of the course most effectively. It offers suggestions for further exploitation in the classroom and self-study time, and contains extra, photocopiable materials for negotiating practice.

The approach

In each unit, *Effective Negotiating* first illustrates a poor model of negotiating practice in order to demonstrate what can go wrong and how (*Version 1*). It then moves on to look at a good model in which the negotiators communicate effectively and progress is made (*Version 2*). The video is essential as the starting point for each unit. The approach is designed to develop learners' abilities in three main areas.

Communication skills

The course develops the key skills which make negotiations successful. It seeks to build the learner's confidence in their ability to deal with all stages of the negotiating process. Skills such as opening the negotiation, establishing your position, dealing with conflict, making proposals, bargaining, and consolidating your position and concluding are demonstrated on the video. These are then analysed and practised with the support of the Student's Book. Learners are encouraged to develop their own style of negotiating based on an awareness of their own particular strengths and weaknesses.

Culture and tactics

In order to develop the learner's awareness of how cultural background can affect negotiating styles and tactics, the course highlights and contrasts certain key communication styles – including, for example, task- versus person-orientation and emotional versus neutral response. The video demonstrates the problems arising when opposing cultural styles clash, whilst the follow-up tasks guide the learner into an analysis of the communication styles fostered by his/her business culture. These concepts are then used to develop the learner's flexibility in dealing with negotiating partners from different cultures.

Language knowledge

Language areas such as sequencing, asking questions, making suggestions, threatening, and making conditions are presented and practised in the Student's Book. The audio cassette is used to further illustrate and practise these areas. Additional exercises at the end of the section seek to develop the listening skills with new language. The exercises at the end of the section provide an opportunity for learners to practise key language functions and structures and to develop their negotiating vocabulary.

Using the course

All parts of the course (except the *Negotiating practice*) are designed to work either as classroom material or for self-study.

In the classroom

Each unit takes the learner through the objectives in the areas of *Communication skills, Culture and tactics, Language knowledge,* and *Negotiating practice.* There is an introduction designed to make the learner think about his/her own experience and to anticipate the focus of the material which follows. Depending on the needs of the group or the amount of time available, the course can be followed from start to finish, or learners can concentrate on selected units. The *Negotiating practice* activities in the Student's Book provide relevant, context-based practice of the key aspects of the unit. These activities are designed for either pairs or small groups. Wherever possible, they should be recorded on audio or video cassette to enable both teacher and learners to analyse and correct the learner's performance when the tape is played back.

Self-study

The video-based activities focusing on communication skills have been developed with the classroom in mind. However, most of the questions have answers in the Answer Key, and individuals can use the video on a self-access basis. The *Culture and tactics* section usually provides some reading input, followed by questions for discussion, self-assessment, or just food for thought. The *Language knowledge* section is ideally suited for self-study, since students can correct their exercises by referring to the Answer Key. The *Negotiating practice* section involves pair or group work, although preparation for these activities could also be done during self-study time.

Who's who in *Effective Negotiating*

The company

Levien SA is based in Brussels, Belgium. It is an international company which manufactures specialist paints and dyes. In its head office it has a small IT function which the company has decided to outsource.

The company

Okus IT are based in Swindon, in the South of England. They specialize in managing IT projects and taking over the IT departments of their client companies.

The people

Françoise Quantin
is the current IT Manager at Levien. She is about to be promoted to Head of Logistics. She is keen that her IT team are protected.

Sean Morrissey
is from Levien's main subsidiary in Chicago. He has been sent to the Brussels Office to develop Levien's procurement policy.

The people

Andrew Carter
is Export Sales Manager for Okus IT. He has been recently recruited by Okus to strengthen their marketing effort outside Britain. He made the initial contact with Levien.

Karen Black
is a Project Manager at Okus IT. She has prepared the specifications for this contract. This is the first time she has been involved in negotiating an overseas outsourcing contract.

The negotiation

Okus have sent a detailed written proposal to Levien. The meeting has been arranged to negotiate the terms of any agreement. In particular the following two issues are likely to be sticking points.

1 Staffing
Levien would like to protect the jobs of their current IT team. They want Okus to employ the four members of the team, and are under pressure from the unions to make sure outsourcing contracts like this do not lead to redundancies.
Okus, on the other hand, will not want to take on Levien's whole team. They already have project engineers based in Swindon.

2 Pricing
Okus have proposed two levels of IT support.
Level A: A fixed monthly price which will cover all support work (daily maintenance and customer support) and specified project work (hardware and software upgrades, training, etc.).
Level B: A lower monthly invoice based on just support work. Any additional project work will be logged and then added to the invoice the following month.
As the video begins, Andrew and Karen have arrived at Levien's offices and are waiting to meet Françoise and Sean.

1 Preparing the ground

Objectives

Communication skills	agreeing objectives, strategy, and roles
Culture and tactics	task-orientation versus people-orientation
Language knowledge	welcome and introductions, negotiating idioms
Negotiating practice	preparing and making opening introductions

Communication skills

Pre-viewing

1 What types of negotiation do you participate in? How would you define a 'negotiation'?

2 How can you prepare for a negotiation? What issues do you need to discuss beforehand?

3 Read the Video Negotiating Context.

Video Negotiating Context

The people

Andrew Carter
is Export Sales Manager for Okus IT. He made the initial contact with Levien. He has met one of the Levien team – Sean – before.

Karen Black
is a Project Manager at Okus IT. She has prepared the specifications for this contract. This is the first time she has been involved in negotiating an overseas outsourcing contract. She is anxious about the meeting.

Françoise Quantin
is the current IT Manager at Levien. She is about to be promoted to Head of Logistics. She is keen that her IT team are protected.

Sean Morrissey
is from Levien's Chicago office. He has been sent to the Brussels office to develop Levien's procurement policy.

The negotiation

Andrew and Karen have arrived at Levien's offices and are waiting to meet Françoise and Sean.

Viewing	▶ 4	Watch Version 1. How confident are you that the negotiation will go well?
	▶ 5	Watch Version 1 again from the beginning to the point where the Levien team enter. How could Karen and Andrew have improved their preparation?
	▶ 6	Watch Version 1 from the entry of the Levien team through to the end. If you were the host, how would you welcome your guests?
	▶ 7	Watch Version 2. How do the two teams establish a more positive atmosphere?
	▶ 8	Watch Version 2 from the entry of the Levien team through to the end. How does Françoise manage the introductions?
Post-viewing	9	How can you prepare effectively for a negotiation? Work in pairs or small groups and brainstorm your ideas. Use the four headings below to help you draw up a preparation checklist for negotiating. When you have finished, compare your checklist with the one in the Answer Key on page 68.

– Objectives   – Roles
– Strategies   – Communication

Culture and tactics

1 Work in pairs. Each of you should read one of the texts below. Prepare to present a summary of the text in your own words to your partner.

Task-oriented

Classically American business culture is very task- or achievement-oriented. In the video, Sean reinforces this stereotype. He doesn't want to waste time with the social niceties; he wants to get down to business. Another way of classifying this type of approach is to say that it is very *specific**. People who adopt this approach tend to focus hard on specific issues – this should mean that time is saved and objectives reached most effectively. However, there is always a danger that the larger picture may be missed and that personal issues can be ignored. These personal issues may be the ones which make or break the deal!

People-oriented

Françoise and Karen reveal themselves as more people-oriented in this first unit. In this respect, they reinforce gender stereotypes from which we expect women to be more aware of people's feelings. Françoise gives time to some small talk before the meeting starts because she believes this will improve communication and lay the basis for possible future relationships. Another way of looking at this is to call it *diffuse**. A diffuse approach to business will place great importance on all the events which surround the actual discussion of the deal. For example, lunch together, social conversation on the way to the airport, or a chance to meet your partner's family.

2   How do you see yourself?

Use the questionnaire below to find out. Tick one or the other of the following statements. If you can't decide, tick neither.

a i   I start the day with a list of things to do.

  ii I start the day by having a chat with my colleagues.

b i   I don't let personal feelings influence decisions.

  ii When making decisions, I look at the human angle first.

c i   If colleagues do a good job, it does not matter if I like them or not.

  ii It's important for me to like the people I work with.

d i   I see meetings only as a means to get business done.

  ii I see meetings partly as an opportunity to develop team relationships.

e i   At the end of the day, I am frustrated if I haven't achieved what I set out to.

  ii At the end of the day, I feel 'low' if I haven't got on with my colleagues.

Scoring: Score 2 points for every **i** sentence you ticked.
       Score 0 points for every **ii** sentence you ticked.
       Score 1 point for every time you ticked neither.

Analysis: 6–10 points   task-oriented
       4–5   points   balanced
       0–3   points   people-oriented

* see acknowledgement on page 2

Language knowledge

'Sorry to have kept you waiting. You must be Karen Black. I'm Françoise Quantin and this is Sean Morrissey.'

1   Listen to the extracts. Match them to the situations below.

Situations

a An informal negotiation between a customer and salesman who know each other well.   ____

b An internal negotiation between a boss and a subordinate about promotion and salary.   ____

c A formal joint-venture negotiation between two international companies.   ____

d An informal negotiation between colleagues.   ____

⌑ 2 Listen again to Extract one. Note down the expressions used to do the following:

    a Welcome visitors/guests – Chairman: _____

    b Introduce yourself/your position – Peter: _____

    c Introduce yourself/your position – Ulrike: _____

    d Introduce a colleague 1 – Yves: _____

    e Introduce a colleague 2 – Yves: _____

⌑ 3 Listen again to Extracts two, three, and four. In each case note down the expression used to switch from small talk subjects to business.

    a Extract two _____

    b Extract three _____

    c Extract four _____

Language focus Welcome, introductions, and small talk

Welcoming

Formal
On behalf of ..., I'm very glad to welcome you ...
It's a pleasure to see you here.

Less formal
Welcome to ...
Thank you for coming all this way.
It's nice to be here.

Greetings

Formal
How do you do.
Nice to meet you.

Less formal
How are you?
Good to see you (again).

Introductions

This is ... He's in charge of ...
*   He looks after ...*
*   He's our ... Director/Manager.*
Let me introduce you to ...
Have you met ...? She's just taken over as Head of ...

Small talk

Did you have a good journey?
How was your flight?
Is this your first visit to ...?
Is your hotel comfortable?

Starting the negotiation

I wondered if I could start by saying ...
We're short of time, so let's get started ...
We've got a very full agenda, so perhaps we'd better get down to business.

4 Speaking practice

Work in groups of four. Two of you are hosts, and two of you are visitors. The visitors have arrived at the hosts' company for a meeting. The hosts need to greet and welcome them.

Host 1 – You already know Visitor 2.
Host 2 – This is the first time that you have met either of the visitors.
Visitor 1 – This is the first time that you have met either of the hosts.
Visitor 2 – You already know Host 1.

Go through the following steps, the hosts initiating the contact, the visitors responding appropriately. When you have finished, change roles.

a Welcome the visitors to the company.
b Greet the visitor you know.
c Allow the visitor you know to introduce his/her colleague to you.
d Introduce your colleague.
e Ask about the visitors' trip.
f Offer the visitors a drink.
g Get down to business.

5 Listen and respond in the following situations.

a You are being welcomed to a meeting with a potential customer.
b You are being introduced to one of the customer's managers.
c You are being asked about the weather.
d You are being asked about your flight.
e You are being asked about your hotel.
f The customer suggests you need to start the meeting.

6

In the video, we saw Andrew and Karen discuss tactics before the Levien team arrived. Watch the dialogue between Karen and Andrew again (both versions). Listen for how the expressions in italics below are used. Then match each expression with its meaning from the right-hand column.

a He *drives a hard bargain.*   i stuck in detail
b You need to *be on your guard.*   ii see what happens
c We're getting *bogged down.*   iii is a tough negotiator
d They'll try to *knock us down.*   iv a bargaining zone
e What's our *fall-back position?*   v contingency plan
f Shall we *play it by ear?*   vi ready to defend your position
g We've got *room to manoeuvre.*   vii reduce our prices

7

Use the appropriate form of one of the expressions in italics in **a–g** above to complete the sentences below.

a It's difficult to predict what's going to happen. I think we should just

_____.

b We've really got _____ in detail and lost sight of our overall objectives.

c We could end up losing money on the contract if we are not careful. The chief negotiator on the other team is very experienced and always

_____.

d Our margins are very tight. There's very little _____.

e I know they think we are charging too much, but if they try
to _____ on price, we're going to have to insist on better
payment terms.

f They are very persuasive negotiators and will throw a lot of impressive-
sounding figures at you, so you should _____.

g Ideally the new buildings will be nearer the airport, but if that proves too
expensive, or there is nothing available, our _____ is to site
the factory here.

Negotiating practice

Pair work

Use the negotiation preparation checklist on page 68 to prepare to
negotiate in each of the following situations. Then carry out the
negotiation, using the checklist. For each situation, you should reach a
conclusion or decision.

Negotiation 1

Student A

You want to sell your car. You have put the advertisement below in the local
paper.

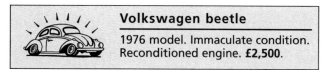

Volkswagen beetle
1976 model. Immaculate condition.
Reconditioned engine. **£2,500.**

Student B

You want to buy a car. You have seen the advertisement above in the local
paper.

Negotiation 2

Student A

You want to buy a second-hand computer. You have seen the advertisement
below in the local paper.

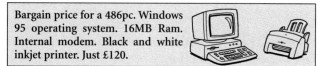

Bargain price for a 486pc. Windows
95 operating system. 16MB Ram.
Internal modem. Black and white
inkjet printer. Just £120.

Student B

You want to sell your computer. You have put the advertisement above in
the local paper.

Negotiation 3

Student A

You are at a meeting with your colleague, Student B, in San Francisco. You both have to travel to another meeting in Los Angeles (which is about 615 km down the coast) in two days' time. You think it would be a good idea to hire a car together and drive there.

Student B

You are at a meeting with your colleague, Student A, in San Francisco. You both have to travel to another meeting in Los Angeles (which is about 615 km down the coast) in two days' time. You think that the best way for the two of you to travel is by plane.

Group work 1 (groups of 4)

Use the negotiation checklist on page 68 to help you prepare to negotiate in the following situations. Then carry out the negotiation, using the checklist. For each situation you should reach a conclusion or decision.

Negotiation 1

Two of you would like to ban all smoking in your offices. Two of you would like to smoke where you want.

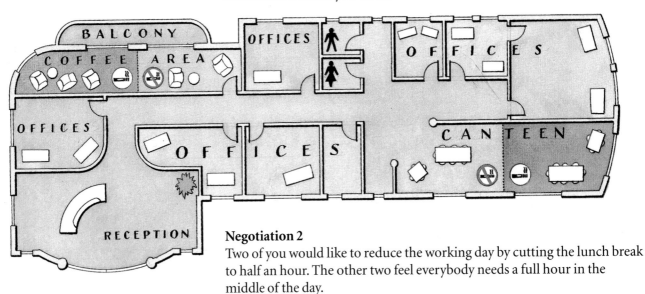

Negotiation 2

Two of you would like to reduce the working day by cutting the lunch break to half an hour. The other two feel everybody needs a full hour in the middle of the day.

Option 1
(current working day)

8.30	start work
12.30	
LUNCH	
13.30	
17.30	finish work

Option 2
(proposed working day)

8.30	start work
12.30	
LUNCH	
13.00	
17.00	finish work

Negotiation 3

Two of you would like to change the office environment to an open-plan working area, where nobody has a fixed desk. The other two would like to retain the present system where all managers have their own offices.

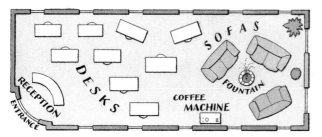 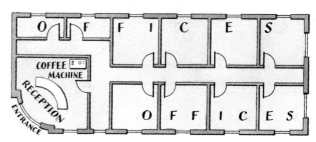

Group work 2 (groups of 4 or 6)

Take roles in the following situations and practise the opening phase of a negotiation. Begin with the hosts welcoming the visitors. Make sure everyone is introduced to each other. Make some polite small talk, and then get down to business by formally opening negotiations.

Negotiation 1

Martenson Consumer Goods manufacture electrical goods such as irons and food mixers. They are looking for a new supplier for some electronic components. They have received an offer from Graziola Electronics, which looks good on paper. The negotiating teams have not previously met but have spoken on the telephone to arrange a meeting. The meeting takes place at Martenson's offices.

The customers (2)

You are Purchasing and Production Managers with Martenson Consumer Goods. It is your responsibility to find a suitable supplier of electronic components. You are hosting the meeting with Graziola Electronics where you will discuss their offer.

The suppliers (2)

You are Sales and Technical Support Representatives with Graziola Electronics. You have come to the meeting to discuss your proposal in more detail.

Negotiation 2

The negotiating team of Ross Financial Services Group have flown into town to negotiate a renewal of a licensing agreement with Weintraub Financial Products PLC. The two teams have met once, a year ago, when the initial deal was struck.

The customers (3)

You are partners in Ross Financial Services Group. You have come to the meeting to discuss renewing your licensing agreement with Weintraub.

The suppliers (3)

You are, respectively, the Product Manager, the Legal Advisor, and the Marketing Director of Weintraub Financial Products PLC. You are hosting the meeting with Ross. You hope to continue supplying them with your financial products.

2 Setting the agenda

Objectives

Communication skills	**structuring and controlling the negotiation process**
Culture and tactics	**organic versus systematic working cultures**
Language knowledge	**sequencing and linking**
Negotiating practice	**controlling the negotiation process**

Communication skills

Pre-viewing

1 Do you think all negotiations need an agenda? Who should be responsible for chairing/controlling a negotiation?

2 Read the Video Negotiating Context.

Video Negotiating Context

The people

Andrew Carter
is Export Sales Manager for Okus IT. He is ready to make his opening presentation.

Karen Black
is a Project Manager at Okus IT. She is expecting Françoise to set out the agenda for the meeting.

Françoise Quantin
is the current IT Manager at Levien. She is very anxious about protecting the jobs of her IT team.

Sean Morrissey
is from Levien's Chicago office. He wants to establish a clear and strong position for Levien.

The negotiation

Andrew and Karen are expecting Françoise, who is chairing the negotiation, to fix the agenda and procedure for the day.

Viewing

▶ 3 Watch Version 1. Why does the negotiation get off to such a bad start?

▶ 4 Watch Version 1 again. Do you think it's a good idea to raise the critical issue so early in the negotiation? How would you handle the aggressive position immediately adopted by Sean?

▶ 5 Watch Version 2. How does Françoise control this opening phase?

▶ 6 Watch Version 2 again. Identify and make a list of the steps which Françoise goes through to open the meeting and set the agenda.

Post-viewing

7 Complete the checklist for opening a negotiation by matching the questions to the appropriate headings. Add any other points you think are important. When you have finished, compare your checklist with the one in the Answer Key on page 71.

Opening negotiation checklist

a Introductions/roles
b Purpose/objectives
c Agenda/structure
d Timing (including breaks)
e Procedure/process

What are the arrangements for breaks/meals?   ___
What are the critical issues?   ___
Who is present?   ___
Will there be presentations/question-and-answer sessions?   ___
Are we going to take minutes?   ___
What roles do the participants have in the negotiation?   ___
Are we going to chair this negotiation?   ___
What are the shared expectations?   ___
How long do we have?   ___
How are we going to start and finish?   ___

Culture and tactics

Karen expects Françoise to be organized and systematic in her approach to the negotiation. This expectation is based on her perception of how best to achieve her objectives. She wants an ordered agenda in which there is an opportunity to go through the main issues step by step. In fact, Françoise lives up to this expectation in the second version.

1 Think about your own approach to negotiation. Where would you place yourself on this continuum?

| chaotic | unstructured | flexible | methodical | systematic |
| impulsive | prepared to take risks | creative | cautious | inflexible |

So-called *universalist** cultures are ones in which people believe there is a right way to do something and, once this has been decided, this procedure should always be followed.

On the other hand, *particularist** cultures are ones in which people believe you need to adapt to each situation differently, and therefore the procedure will have to be changed according to the situation.

2 What sort of working culture (universalist or particularist) do you think characterizes these companies?

a **Crantons Engineering**
An old-fashioned family engineering firm employing 1,400 workers. Run along traditional lines. Quite hierarchical and rather slow in decision-making. Very sound finance.

b **Gilson, Merritt, and Partners**
A management consultancy partnership employing twenty-five staff. Young and dynamic. Very team-oriented. Has responded well to market changes.

c **ATZO**
A large chemical multinational. Formed by the merger of an Italian pharmaceutical company and a German speciality chemicals company. Bureaucratic and rather unresponsive to market changes.

d **COMinternational**
A medium-sized financial services group. A strong reputation for financial management and control systems. Run by charismatic CEO Jesper Jonsson.

3 How would you describe the culture of the place that you work for? Make a short presentation to the rest of the group comparing two work cultures (e.g. your previous versus your current employer).

* see acknowledgment on page 2

Language knowledge

'I'd like to start by saying a few words about the meeting today and what we expect to achieve ...'

1 Listen to these negotiation openings. Which of the following steps do they include? (Tick (✓) the appropriate columns.)

Extract	introduction	objectives	agenda	timing	roles	procedures
one						
two						
three						
four						
five						
six						

[cassette] **2** Listen again and answer the questions.

    a Extract one: what's on the agenda before and after lunch?
    b Extract two: what's the first issue to be discussed?
    c Extract three: why should they cooperate?
    d Extract four: in what way will the agreement change?
    e Extract five: what's on the agenda after lunch?
    f Extract six: how long will today's meeting last?

Language focus   Sequencing and linking

Objectives

We're here today to ...
The main objective/purpose of today's meeting is ...
We're looking to achieve ...

Agenda

We've drawn up an agenda.
Let's just run through the agenda.
There are two/three/four items on the agenda.
I'd like to take ... first.
We've put ... last.
Let's leave ... until later.
We aim to deal with/cover ... under item three.

Timing

That gives us two hours.
It will take two hours.
It won't take long.
I need to be away by ... o'clock.
How are you fixed for time?

Roles

... is going to sit in.
... is going to take the minutes.
... would like to say a few words about ...
... you're going to give us a presentation.

Procedure

We'll deal with ... first.
We'll go round the table.
We'll have a question and answer session at the end.
We can table that for discussion later.

---

3 Complete the following sentences with the correct form of one of the verbs from the list below.

run	*take*	*put*	*come*	*give*	*go*

    a Can we just _____ through the agenda?
    b It won't _____ more than a couple of minutes.
    c It would be easier if we _____ the question of staff first.
    d Don't worry. John will _____ the minutes.
    e Françoise is going to _____ a brief presentation.
    f Then we can _____ round the table.
    g We'll _____ to that in a moment.
    h I think we should _____ that last.
    i So, that _____ us just half an hour.

4 Speaking practice

Work in small groups. Choose one of the three negotiating scenarios below and prepare the opening. Use the preparation checklist to help you. When you are ready, take it in turns to be the chairperson and open the negotiation – remember to use appropriate sequencing and linking expressions.

a

Objective	to reach agreement about terms for a new annual printing contract
Agenda	1 existing contract – advantages and disadvantages
	2 problem of delivery times
	3 new contract – main elements
Timing	10.00 – 16.00 (lunch booked)
Roles	Peter: minutes
	Margarita: present new contract
Procedure	opening presentation by printing company.

b

Objective	to settle a dispute over bonuses with the union
Agenda	1 financial update
	2 salary grades
	3 new bonus system
Timing	morning (the following day if necessary)
Roles	Frank Raguzzi: chief negotiator
	Sandip Mullah: assistant, minute-taker
Procedure	you will start by presenting a financial update.

c

Objective	to negotiate terms for a large loan
Agenda	1 past financial record
	2 business plan
	3 financing requirements
Timing	break for lunch at 12.30
Roles	Mr Mohar, Financial Advisor: to deal with specific questions.

5 a Below are some constructions used in 'weighing up' – or comparing the negative and positive aspects of an issue. Fill in the blanks.

a pros   and _____

b _____ and disadvantages

c strengths   and _____

d _____ and minuses

b Fill in the blanks using words from above, and then make a brief presentation about one of the following.

'The pros and _____ of getting married.'

'The _____ and disadvantages of living in a city.'

'The _____ and minuses of being self-employed.'

'The strengths and _____ of my English!'

6 Here are a series of negotiating idioms using the word *ground*. Match the idioms in italics (**a-i**) with equivalent expressions (**i-ix**) below.

  a You're *on dangerous ground.*
  b We need to *find some common ground.*
  c We've *covered a lot of ground.*
  d You must *keep both feet on the ground.*
  e You're *on shaky ground* there.
  f We're just *going over the same ground.*
  g Their offer *cut the ground from under us.*
  h Don't give in. *Hold your ground.*
  i We have *lost ground* to our competitors.

  i   dealt with a lot of points
  ii   repeating ourselves
  iii undermined our position
  iv   there's a high risk of failure
  v   don't make any concessions
  vi   your arguments are not very convincing
  vii points we can agree on
  viii we're in a weaker position
  ix   be cautious and sensible

7 Which of the idiomatic expressions from a–i above would you use in the following situations?

  a Our sales have gone down sharply this year, whilst our competitors have increased their market share.
  b You have had a day of wide-ranging discussion, and have talked through many of the issues on your agenda.
  c A rival company has made a competitive bid which makes your offer look really expensive.
  d You must stand firm. You cannot afford to make any more concessions.
  e You are looking for areas of agreement.
  f The negotiation has got stuck and is not moving forward. At the moment, all you are doing is repeating yourselves.
  g There is a risk that you could be seduced into making a silly offer. You must proceed very carefully.
  h You need to be very cautious in this particular area of the negotiation.

Negotiating practice

Group work (groups of 4)

Use the checklist on page 71 to prepare for the start of the following negotiations. Prepare in pairs and then practise the opening. When you have finished, change roles.

Negotiation 1

The buyers (2)

Your company is called Saroyan-Arttech. You manufacture toys. You have invited a training firm to a meeting to discuss taking over some of the management training in your company. This training is currently done by in-house trainers, but the plan is to outsource all training in the future. You have seen their brochures and course descriptions. Their quoted prices are very high and you would like to see if you can negotiate lower prices for a commitment to a number of courses. You are looking for at least twenty per cent reduction for the promise of twenty-five days of training.

The sellers (2)

You run a management training consultancy. You have sent your brochures (prices and course descriptions) to Saroyan-Arttech. You have been invited to attend a meeting to discuss your services. You know that they are planning to outsource all their training. You hope that the meeting will be an opportunity to present your services in detail and to discuss particular courses.

Negotiation 2

The buyers (2)

You are purchasers for Futura, a large manufacturing company. You have recently organized a call for tenders for the supply of packaging material. You have shortlisted three companies. One of them is DTX Packaging, with whom you have arranged this meeting. The objective is to clarify delivery and payment terms, as well as to discuss penalty clauses for late delivery or below-standard quality.

The sellers (2)

You represent DTX Packaging. You have been invited to discuss an offer you made for the supply of packaging material to Futura. You understand the meeting is designed to clarify elements of your offer – including payment terms and delivery periods. You would also like to discuss price discounts for large quantities.

Negotiation 3

The buyers (2)

You represent the Koruna Hotel group, which owns a small chain of hotels in Northern Europe. In order to conform to new European regulations regarding health and hygiene, you need to replace all the heavy-duty dishwashers used in your hotel kitchens. Luxicon, a company which manufactures catering equipment, have made you a proposal for the supply and maintenance of new dishwashers. You have invited them to your head office to discuss a possible contract. You need to clarify payment and delivery terms, and negotiate the maintenance contract to ensure that it includes regular servicing for all the machines as well as emergency repair work. Since Luxicon supplied some of your old dishwashers, you want to discuss the possibility of some kind of part-exchange deal, whereby they can take away your old machines and give you a discount on the new ones.

The sellers (2)

You represent Luxicon, a large manufacturing company which makes kitchen equipment for hotels and restaurants. You have been invited to the headquarters of the Koruna hotel group to discuss your offer for the supply and maintenance of new heavy-duty dishwashers for all their hotel kitchens. The issues to be negotiated will include payment and delivery terms, and the conditions of the maintenance contract. You know that new European hygiene regulations will oblige Koruna to replace other items of catering equipment as well as their dishwashers. You want to discuss the possibility of offering a discount in return for an exclusive contract to supply Koruna hotels with all their kitchen equipment.

3 Establishing positions

Objectives

Communication skills	**presenting your position, getting feedback**
Culture and tactics	**direct versus indirect communication**
Language knowledge	**asking for and giving feedback**
Negotiating practice	**establishing positions**

Communication skills

Pre-viewing

1   When you present your position, what do you hold back?

2   What is the best way to make sure you get feedback on your position?

3   Read the Video Negotiating Context.

Video Negotiating Context

The people

Andrew Carter
is Export Sales Manager for Okus IT. He has prepared a presentation of the key aspects of their offer.

Karen Black
is a Project Manager at Okus IT. She is expecting Andrew to present their offer.

Françoise Quantin
is the current IT Manager at Levien. She is expecting Andrew to identify key aspects of their offer.

Sean Morrissey
is from Levien's Chicago office. He'd like to hear what they are offering in terms of staffing levels.

The negotiation

Andrew is going to present the Okus position and get feedback from Levien. He knows that there are two issues which will dominate the negotiations:

1 Staffing levels Levien would like Okus to take on all its existing IT team. Okus need to resist this pressure.

2 Support levels Okus have proposed a choice of support levels.
Level A: The price includes full support and a certain amount of project work, to be specified in advance.

Level B: The price includes full support, but no project work. Project work will be invoiced separately, as and when it occurs.

Viewing

▶ 4 Watch Version 1. What do you think of Andrew's presentation style?

▶ 5 Watch Version 1 again. Think of ways in which Andrew could respond more to the needs of Levien?

▶ 6 Watch Version 2. How has Andrew's style changed?

▶ 7 Watch Version 2 again. Make a list of the different ways in which Andrew involves the Levien team in his presentation.

Post-viewing

8 Make a short presentation on one of the topics below. Make sure you get feedback and involvement from the rest of the group during the presentation. Be prepared for any questions they might ask you.

– Why you shouldn't drink and drive.
– Town or country: the best place to live.
– Why you should buy my car.
– Where we should eat tonight (your favourite restaurant).
– The best film I've ever seen.
– Why women live longer than men.
– Which charity you should support.

Culture and tactics

Andrew frustrates Sean because he seems slow in coming to the point. A fundamental difference between British and American styles of communication is directness. In British negotiations, especially at the early stages, people would not say: 'What I really want to know is: are you going to hire our staff or not?' Something like: 'I'm interested to know what your position on our staff is,' would be preferred.

People from cultures which favour direct communication would probably find this lack of directness unhelpful: they believe in saying what they think. On the other hand, more indirect cultures might find the direct style abrasive and unsubtle. Indirect cultures are worried that the direct statement or question may put your partner 'on the spot' (under pressure), and could lead to loss of face if he or she is unable to respond.

For someone from a direct culture, the main problem is understanding the real question or point behind a rather vague expression – in other words, 'reading between the lines'.

1 What is the more direct question or statement behind these sentences?

a I'd be interested to know more about your prices.
b That figure looks a little on the high side.
c Delivery is an area which we'd like to explore a little further with you.
d I'd like to know more about your management structure.
e It's true that marketing is one of the things we are worried about.

2 Indirectness is achieved by making questions and statements vague and not too specific. Try making the following questions and statements vaguer.

   a I don't like your forecasts.
   b How do you plan to do that?
   c I want to know about payment terms.
   d Your costs are too high.
   e How much will you charge?

Language knowledge

'Perhaps you'd like to talk to our clients in Edinburgh?'

 1 Listen to these extracts from negotiators presenting their position. Decide whether you think they are *talking at* their audience, or *talking with* them. (Tick (✔) the appropriate column.)

Extract	talking at	talking with
one		
two		
three		
four		

2 Listen again and identify the features which made two of the extracts more interactive. (Tick (✔) the appropriate space.)

Extract	one	two	three	four
inviting to interrupt				
negotiating agenda				
considering what they already know				
checking for agreement				
use of *we/let's*				

Language focus Asking for and giving feedback

Inviting interruptions

Please don't hesitate to interrupt.
Please feel free to ask questions.
Let's deal with any questions immediately.
I/We would like to know what you think.

Negotiating the agenda

Let's just identify the key issues.
Shall we look at ... first?
Perhaps we should consider ... first?
We see two/three important issues ... Would you agree?
If I understand correctly, you're interested in ...

Considering what they already know

You've all seen our brochures/proposal/offer.
I think you've all had a chance to read our ...
I don't want to go over the same ground.

Checking for agreement/approval

Formal
Would/wouldn't you agree that ...?
Do you mind if ...
I hope you don't mind if ...
Could I/we ...?

Less formal
If that's all right with you?
Is that OK?

NOTE Use of *we/let's* rather than *I/you.*

Where possible, it's more inclusive to say *We'd like to ...* (rather than *I'd like to ...*) or, *Let's start by talking about ...* (rather than *I'd like to start by talking about ...*). Certainly if you are a member of a team, use *we* rather than *I*.

---

3   Change or add to these sentences so that they do not just state what you want, but invite your negotiating partner's opinion. Encourage him/her to give you feedback.

For example:
I would like to make an early start.
Would it be OK if we started early? or, *Could we start early?*

a   I want to finish at five.
b   Miss Higa will sit in during the negotiation.
c   I think we should take a break now.
d   These are the three areas I want to cover this morning.
e   I'd like to go through the written offer clause by clause.
f   I'll answer your questions at the end.

4   Make these statements into proposals and suggestions. Be inclusive – use *we* rather than *I*. Try to word your sentences so that they encourage feedback.

For example:
I think that a date should be set for the next meeting.
Wouldn't you agree that we need to set a date for the next meeting?
or, *Perhaps we should set a date for the next meeting?*

a   I think we should start by looking at the rising production costs.
b   I think that timing is essential. Don't you?
c   It's important to identify who our main competitors are first.
d   I would prefer to discuss transport issues at the end.
e   It's your computer system which is causing the problem.

5 Speaking practice

Work in pairs. Take it in turns to make brief introductions to the following negotiating situations. Make sure you invite feedback as often as possible. Your partner should listen, respond when appropriate, and criticize. When you have finished, change roles.

a You need to establish your position as a strong contender for an exclusive licence. You are at the start of the negotiation with the manufacturer.

> i Suggest agenda: two areas – (1) finance, (2) marketing.
> ii Invite interruptions.
> iii Mention the written proposal you have already sent.
> iv Suggest that you point out key financial advantages of your offer.
> v Check agreement.

b You want to establish your position as a supplier of office equipment. You are at the start of a negotiation with a large wholesaler.

> i Suggest agenda: three key items – (1) quality, (2) delivery, (3) payment.
> ii Invite interruptions.
> iii Mention the client references you have already sent.
> iv Suggest you start by going through catalogue.
> v Check agreement.

c You want to negotiate a better salary with your boss. You are at the start of the meeting and you want to establish the reasons why you should get a rise.

> i Suggest agenda: two areas – (1) performance, (2) promotion opportunities.
> ii Mention appraisal report which he or she should have already read.
> iii Check agreement.

Negotiating practice

Group work 1 Selling your company

Each member of the group should make a presentation about his/her company, integrating techniques and language which involve the audience. Choose from the topics below or, if you prefer, choose your own. The rest of the group are prospective customers. Be prepared to answer any questions they might ask.

- Your company's products/services
- Your company's customer service benefits
- Your company versus the competition
- Your company's track record (e.g. client references)

Group work 2 Selling a product, a service, or an idea

In your groups choose one of the topics below. Each member of the group should prepare a short presentation to sell his/her version of the product, service, or idea, integrating techniques and language which involve the audience. The rest of the group are the prospective customers. Be prepared to answer any questions they might ask.

- A holiday destination (e.g. in your country)
- A job opportunity (e.g. in your company)
- New technology (e.g. Internet application)
- A new management idea (e.g. organization, change, training, etc.)

4 Clarifying positions

Objectives

Communication skills	**active listening, effective questioning**
Culture and tactics	**individuals versus teams**
Language knowledge	**asking questions, showing interest**
Negotiating practice	**active listening tasks**

Communication skills

Pre-viewing

1   In a negotiation, what are the advantages to be gained from listening well? What can stop you from listening?

2   How can you ensure that: a you listen effectively to others?
                              b others listen effectively to you?

3   Read the Video Negotiating Context.

Video Negotiating Context

The people

Andrew Carter
is Export Sales Manager for Okus IT. He is ready to support Karen, if she needs it.

Karen Black
is a Project Manager at Okus IT. She is hoping to clarify some of the details of the Okus offer.

Françoise Quantin
is the current IT Manager at Levien. She is worried about the fees for project management.

Sean Morrissey
is from Levien's Chicago office. He is concerned about the level of support they will get from Okus.

The negotiation

Karen is trying to clarify the options which Okus has proposed. Essentially there are two levels of support:

Level A: A complete package: all support work and projects specified at the start of the year are included in the monthly invoice. Levien consider this a very expensive option.

Level B: A cheaper option: the monthly invoice will include all support work but no project work; any project work would be logged by the engineers and then charged at an hourly rate the following month.

Levien do not like this option because they feel it is open to abuse – who will decide what is support work and what is project work?

Viewing

▷ 4 Watch Version 1. Why does Karen get so frustrated?

▷ 5 Watch Version 1 again. How could Karen ensure that Levien really understand what is on the table?

▷ 6 Watch Version 2. What do you notice about Françoise's participation?

▷ 7 Watch Version 2 again. How does Karen manage the session?

Post-viewing

8 Improve your listening techniques. Complete the questionnaire below and then compare your results with a colleague. What aspects of your listening could you improve?

Effective listening questionnaire

Do you	always	sometimes	never
1 Listen for feelings as well as words?			
2 Follow the topic continuously?			
3 Stop listening when you think the speaker is wrong?			
4 Start planning your response while you are listening?			
5 Let others have the last word?			
6 Consider another point of view before disagreeing?			
7 Make up your mind before starting to listen?			

WHISPER WHISPER

PAUL'S ABILITY TO LISTEN AND PICK UP WHAT OTHERS ARE THINKING IS VERY USEFUL IN CRITICAL NEGOTIATIONS.

Culture and tactics

In the bad version of this negotiation, neither side works as a team. In the good version, not only do they work as teams, they also try to develop a potential new team for the future.

1   How would you describe the dominant attitudes towards leaders and teams at your workplace? There are seven contrasted statements below. Is your work culture more *individualist* or *collectivist*?

Individualist*	Collectivist*
Leaders need to have strong personalities.	Leaders need to be sympathetic to the group.
Individuals come up with the best ideas.	Teams come up with the best ideas.
Some people are not worth listening to.	Everybody is worth listening to.
Decision-making takes twice as long in teams.	Decision-making in teams is the only way to get commitment.
Individuals should be rewarded for their success.	Teams should share their rewards equally.
When something goes wrong, someone must take the blame.	When something goes wrong, the blame should be shared.
The best companies have the best leaders.	The best companies have the best workforce.

* see acknowledgment on page 2

2   In terms of negotiating tactics, which of the following statements would you agree with and why?

   a   One way to break down the opposition is to find differences of opinion or position within the same negotiating team. In other words, 'divide and rule!'

   b   Scoring points off your negotiating partners is finally non-productive. It will only lead to mutual mistrust in the long term.

   c   The best negotiators are fluent communicators, flexible enough to adapt to changing circumstances, but tough enough to withstand pressure when they do not want to make any changes or concessions.

   d   The best negotiators are good listeners. Only by understanding the position and desires of your partners across the table can you come to an agreement which is mutually beneficial.

3   What advice would you give to an inexperienced negotiator?

Language knowledge

*'You pay a set fee and you don't pay
anything extra.'*
*'So, our contract would specify all
IT projects.'*
'No, it's shorter term ...'

 1 Listen to the following extracts. Decide whether people are listening well
or not. (Tick (✓) the appropriate column.)

Extract	listen well	listen badly
one		
two		
three		
four		

 2 Listen again and identify which of these features are present. (Tick (✓) the
appropriate space.)

Extract	one	two	three	four
opportunity to ask questions				
questions on the subject				
questions off the subject				
opportunity to answer question				
no opportunity to answer question				
check answer is satisfactory				
encourage/show interest				

Language focus Asking questions and showing interest

General

I'd be interested to know more about ...
Could you tell us something about ...?

Detailed

What exactly do you mean by ...?
Could you be more specific ...

Supportive

So, you are saying ...
If I understand you correctly, you are offering ...
Am I right in thinking you plan to ...?

Checking answer is satisfactory

Does that answer your question?
Is that clear?

Encouraging/showing interest

Go ahead.   That's interesting.   Fine.
Sure.   Please do.   Of course.

Managing questions

Can I deal with that later?
I was just coming to that.
Could I just finish what I was saying?

3 Listen to the five statements. For each one, ask a general question on the subject.

For example:
statement: The main issue in this contract is timing.
general question: *I'd be interested to know more about the timing.*

a _____

b _____

c _____

d _____

e _____

4 Listen to the five statements. For each one, ask a probing question about detail.

For example:
statement: The sales should peak during the second year.
probing question: *When exactly will they peak?*

a _____

b _____

c _____

d _____

e _____

5 Read between the lines of these brief explanations. For each one, ask a supportive or reflective question.

For example:
explanation: We're going to offer two packages. One at the top end of the market, priced around twenty dollars. The other, a middle-range product, around fifteen dollars and pitched for the mass market.
supportive question: *So, you expect much higher sales on the second product?*

a There are two people who can do this job. Ivan is the obvious candidate. He's got plenty of experience. Then there's Philippa. She's very well liked in the company. But then, she's a woman.

question: _____
(a man?)

b The weather's got worse and we've had to invest more in protecting the plants. We don't like passing on costs to our customers but I'm afraid there's no alternative.

question: _____
(price rise?)

c We're moving to a cheaper part of town so we anticipate that our rent will come down. On the other hand, labour costs have gone up, so it's difficult to be flexible.

question: _____
(offer no discount?)

d Since we outsourced part of the IT function we no longer hold records on all our customers. It's difficult to say very much about this customer's credit rating.

question: _____
(risk doing business?)

e The bid we received from our usual supplier was disappointing. The price they quoted was considerably higher than we had budgeted for.

question: _____
(other supplier?)

6 Listen to the five offers. In each case, make an encouraging response.

For example:
Shall I tell you something about the financing?
Please do.

a _____

b _____

c _____

d _____

e _____

7 **Speaking practice**

Practise using a variety of question types for the following activity.

Student A

You are negotiating a contract for the catering and entertainment for an office party. Your task is to explain the details of the party and then to listen to the offer which Celebration Nights makes.

Student B

You represent Celebration Nights, a business which arranges parties for corporate clients. You have been contacted by Student A who wants to arrange an office party.
Your task is to listen to what Student A plans and to clarify all points, then to present what your company can offer.

Student A   **Student B**

Tell Student B about
the proposed party
(date, time, occasion,
number of guests).

Clarify any points.
Tell Student A what
you can offer (food,
music, drinks, costs).

Clarify any points.

8 The words in italics in the sentences below are all concerned with prices and payment. In each sentence, replace the word in italics with the correct form of one of the words or expressions from the box.

> rate fee invoice ballpark figure discount charge commission

a The consultant's *prices* are astronomical!
b Could you give me a *rough figure* for the conversion?
c When will you be *billing* us ?
d Your hourly *price* seems to be above the industry average.
e How much do you *ask for* per day?
f If you book well in advance, you get a *reduction*.
g The problem is too many people are taking a *percentage of* the final price.

9 You are negotiating with a supplier for the supply of computer hardware and support. Make the following enquiries and suggestions, using words and expressions from the box in **8** above.

a Ask the supplier for a rough idea of how much he plans to charge for the hardware.
b Find out if he receives any bonus on the sale.
c Ask for the bill to be sent with all the others to your offices at the end of the month.
d Find out how much an hour you will have to pay for support.
e Ask whether some reduction can be made considering the size of the order.
f Suggest you don't use lawyers because you have to pay them too much.

Negotiating practice

Pair work

In the following situations, **Student A** should explain or present the information, **Student B** should listen, understand, and be able to summarize what has been said. When you have finished, change roles.

Situation 1
One partner should explain their company/organization's social policy (benefits, holidays, special incentives, etc.). The other should listen, understand, and then summarize.

Situation 2
One partner should explain 'How I learnt English'. The other should listen, understand, and then summarize.

Situation 3
One partner should present a technique or process (IT, personnel, financial, etc.) which he or she uses at work. The other should listen, understand, and then summarize.

Situation 4
One partner should describe their own personal negotiating style. The other should listen, understand, and then summarize.

Group work (groups of 4)

The situation

This is a negotiation between a supplier and a prospective client. The team for the supplier need to ensure they have understood their client's needs. The client's team need to find out as much as they can about what kind of company the supplier is and what they have to offer. After the first meeting, the supplier should draft a written proposal for a contract. The clients must decide if the proposal seems to meet their needs, and whether or not they wish to proceed with the negotiation.

The suppliers (2)

You represent a recruitment agency – Human Potential. You have arranged to meet a potential client – Baylor and Sons. They are a large textile company who are planning to expand their workforce. They are interested in using an agency to look after the recruitment. Your task is to understand their needs, and be able to draw up a written proposal for the contract. The Baylor team may well ask questions about your services. You should prepare answers in the following areas:
– year of foundation
– annual turnover
– main clients
– number of staff
– recruitment fees (% of annual salary).

The customers (2)

You represent Baylor and Sons, a large textile company. You are planning to expand your workforce due to a restructuring of your business. You want to use a recruitment agency to recruit your new staff. You have arranged a meeting with Human Potential. The objective of the meeting is to explain your needs so that they can prepare a full written offer for the contract. You need to prepare a contract to cover the following:
– background to the company
– restructuring
– need for new employees
– proposed wages/salaries
– categories and numbers of employees (textile workers/supervisors/management)
– start dates.

5 Managing conflict

Objectives

Communication skills   avoiding personal criticism
Culture and tactics   conflict versus collaboration
Language knowledge   downtoning your language
Negotiating practice   handling conflict

Communication skills

Pre-viewing

1 What's your view on conflict in a negotiation? What are the risks and the potential benefits?

2 Do you think that conflict should be avoided at all costs? Or does it have a positive role to play?

3 Read the Video Negotiating Context.

Video Negotiating Context

The people

Andrew Carter
is Export Sales Manager for Okus IT. He starts to feel his position is under threat.

Karen Black
is a Project Manager at Okus IT. She is beginning to get a bit frustrated with Sean and even sometimes with Andrew.

Françoise Quantin
is the current IT Manager at Levien. She wants to make sure a positive atmosphere is maintained.

Sean Morrissey
is from Levien's Chicago office. He thinks the negotiation is getting stuck and plans to shake it up.

The negotiation

They are discussing the issue of identifying what is support work and what is project work. If Levien opt for a Level B contract, additional project work will be invoiced on top of the basic contract. Levien feel this is open to abuse and would like to drop the idea of logging additional project work.

▶ 4   Watch Version 1 from the beginning to the point where Karen and Andrew leave the meeting room. Why does Karen call for time-out?

▶ 5   Watch Version 1 from the point where Karen and Andrew leave the meeting room to the end. What do Françoise and Sean disagree about?

▶ 6   Watch Version 2. What's the difference in Sean's approach this time?

▶ 7   Watch Version 2 from the point where Karen and Andrew leave the meeting room to the end. What are Sean and Françoise talking about? What's the difference in their approach?

Post-viewing

8   Which of the following statements do you agree with? Working with a partner, draw up three statements which summarize your own views on the issues addressed here.

Culture and tactics

Sean's approach is very confrontational. He comes from a business culture where aggressive tactics are justified if they achieve their ends. Françoise, on the other hand, comes from a working culture which is much more collaborative, placing importance on harmony.

1 Which of these negotiators do you most identify with?

Sharon Stacey works in Klein and Belaby's International Mergers and Acquisitions group. She has a reputation for being one of their toughest negotiators. She has fought her way up in a male-dominated world and has an assertive style of negotiating. She is very task-orientated and pushes for results as quickly as possible.

Thor Gunnarson has a reputation for being a 'Mr Fix-it'. He speaks six languages and has lived in both the United States and Thailand. He is well liked by all his staff. He has negotiated contracts for a multinational metals company all over the world. He is known for his patience. His negotiating style is slow, deliberate, and aimed at maintaining harmony.

Patrick O'Brien runs his own multinational consultancy company. He has a reputation as a skillful and resourceful negotiator. He always researches in depth before a negotiation and prides himself in being as well prepared as possible. His background is in the law and he is known to have a meticulous eye for legal detail.

Loo Hok is a successful entrepreneur based in Singapore. He always spends time getting to know his business partners and places great value on the strength of family and personal relationships. When it comes to negotiating, he is clear about what he wants to achieve, and will pursue his objectives single-mindedly.

2 Discuss your own negotiating style in terms of your attitude to the following.

- conflict
- personal relationships
- preparation
- time
- concessions

Language knowledge

'Please don't get me wrong. It's the people on the ground I'm worried about.'

1 Listen to the following extracts from negotiations. In each case, decide whether the approach is confrontational or collaborative. (Tick (✓) the appropriate column.)

Extract	confrontational	collaborative
one		
two		
three		
four		

2 Listen again and fill in the gaps to complete the sentences.

a **Extract one** use of threats

If you _____ , sales _____ .

b **Extract two** balanced argument

Well, I can see _____ ,

but we also _____ .

c **Extract two** personalized criticism

Sure, sure, but some _____ .

I mean, _____ ?

d **Extract three** use of *would/could/may*

But I think we'd all agree _____

_____ .

There may be _____

_____ .

Language focus Downtoning your language

Modifiers

Perhaps/Maybe
Perhaps we should consider reducing ...
Maybe you could cut down ...
Perhaps you have more staff than you can really afford.
Maybe we should rethink the question of ...

A bit/just/a little

If you could just offer us ...
That sounds a bit too risky.
I think those figures are a little optimistic.
We need a little bit more time/money.

Use of *would/could/may*

Perhaps we could all think about ...
Wouldn't we all agree that ...?
There may be one or two ...

Use of negatives for modifying

It won't be too expensive if ... (it will be cheaper)
Cutting here will not be too critical . (it will be fine)
It won't take so long if ... (it will be quicker)

Use of *I'm afraid*

I'm afraid your prices are a bit high.
I'm afraid we can't offer any more than that.

  NOTE ON INTONATION

Intonation plays a very important role in downtoning. Listen to these pairs of statements spoken with different intonation patterns.

1 *Your prices are a bit high.* (single pitch, serious)
   Your prices are a bit high. (rising intonation, positive tone)

2 *Wouldn't you agree?* (falling tone, threatening)
   Wouldn't you agree? (rising tone, encouraging)

3 Modify the following remarks using one or more of the techniques above. There may be more than one possible answer.

For example:
Your labour costs are too high.
I'm afraid your labour costs are too high.
Or, *Your labour costs are a bit too high.*

a We must cut the advertising budget.
b PR expenditure is much too high.
c You need to analyse your costs in more detail.
d There is no room for any cuts in my budget.
e Don't you agree we should cut this budget?
f You should read the proposal properly.
g Look at page thirty-two of the document.
h How can you make such a poor offer?

4 Use opposite adjectives to soften the following remarks.

For example:
This is a very unproductive meeting.
This meeting could be a bit more productive.

a This is the worst food I've ever tasted.
b Don't be so late tomorrow.
c How can your forecasts be so unreliable?
d You really are very inexperienced.
e Your quotation is much too expensive.
f Your financial position is insecure.

5 Speaking practice

a Modify this dialogue so that it sounds less confrontational.

b Record your new version.

c Compare your new version with the two versions on the cassette, one spoken with more positive intonation.

A: Your figures for last year look bad.

B: No, they're not.

A: I don't think we can do business on this basis.

B: Why not?

A: Because your track record is not strong enough.

B: I can't see how you can say that. We have some excellent customer references.

A: None of them have been with you long.

B: That's not true. What about Phoenix International? We've been working with them for five years.

A: That's not what I call long.

B: But we've only been in business for six years!

6 Work with a partner to write a dialogue using the prompts below. There is a conflict between the Production Planning Department and the Purchasing Department due to a large surplus of expensive electrical components lying in the warehouse. Use as many modifying structures as you can to downtone your language and defuse the conflict.

Student A

You are responsible for Production Planning. You cannot understand why your department is paying storage costs for a large quantity of electrical components you do not need. Due to a cancellation of a customer order you recently had to reduce production and you have used fewer components than originally predicted.

Student B

You work in the Purchasing Department. You are responsible for ordering these electrical components, but you calculated the size of the order according to the output schedule given to you to by Production. You always order extra and a long time in advance because these particular components are difficult to get and the orders take a long time to arrive.

Student A

1 Too many components. B over-ordered. Purchasing Dept. is badly organized.

3 Losing money now for storage – Expensive because components are fragile and must be kept in special conditions. Warehouse is crowded. No room for other orders.

5 Purchasing is badly informed. Large customer order was cancelled. Production had to reduce output.

7 Purchasing is unresponsive. Production did not know if the message was received or not.

Student B

2 Production Dept. is badly informed. Ordered extra because there are problems in supply. Long delays waiting for orders. The company loses money.

4 Surplus because Production has not used as many components as it predicted. A's predictions for this year inaccurate.

6 Purchasing received this information too late. Production is too slow at giving information.

8 Production and Purchasing must think of ways to improve communication.

Negotiating practice

Group work 1 (groups of 5)
An internal negotiation – a personnel problem

One year ago, you (the Commercial Director), recruited two young graduates to your division – Elaine Smith and Peter Grange. They have both proved excellent additions to the team. The working atmosphere in the division has always been very relaxed and positive. A few weeks ago everything went sour. David Graham, their direct boss, promoted Peter to the role of Project Leader. Elaine has accused David of discriminating against her because she is a woman. She says she was never considered for promotion and is threatening to take the company to court for breaking the equal opportunities law.

Commercial Director

You have known David for a long time. He's a traditional man and you can imagine that he might favour a male manager. You want to listen to everybody's opinions before resolving this issue. You certainly don't want this issue to go to court.

David Graham (Marketing Manager)

You are angry that Elaine has accused you of discrimination. You feel that Peter was the best person for the job and that is the end of it. You certainly feel you shouldn't give in to Elaine's threats of taking the company to court.

Sales Manager

You have worked with David Graham for ten years. He is an excellent Marketing Manager. However he is not such a good manager of people. You suspect that he did not communicate his decision about this promotion in the right way. He should have involved all the team so that no jealousies arose. You have worked with Elaine and you feel she's very competent and therefore the best solution would be to transfer her to your department.

Human Resources Manager

You sympathize with Elaine. Very few women are promoted in the company. However you think she should not be threatening the company. You think the situation has been caused by poor communication.

Public Relations Manager

You sympathize with David. You have met Elaine and find her rather aggressive. If you had to make the same decision, you would have promoted Peter too.

Group work 2 (groups of 4)
An external negotiation – a question of qualifications

Namaste Pharmaceuticals are negotiating with Atali Healthcare for the use of their sales force to promote a drug which they have recently licensed. The negotiation was going well until the Namaste Marketing Manager discovered that Atali had exaggerated the qualifications of their sales force. In this meeting, the issue will be raised and hopefully resolved.

Namaste Pharmaceuticals

Marketing Manager

While you have been negotiating, you asked a consultancy to look into the background and qualifications of the Atali sales team. You discovered that two of them were not graduates, as specified by Atali. You have no evidence that they are less able, but you feel Atali have overstated the strength of their sales force, and therefore you have started to question the whole deal. You would like a satisfactory explanation. If you don't get one, you are inclined to break off negotiations.

Area Sales Manager

The Atali sales team would be working under you. You can understand why your colleague is so upset, but you feel there is probably a quite innocent explanation. You are very keen for the negotiation to succeed, as you desperately need support for your sales activity.

Atali Healthcare

Marketing Director

You know that the Namaste team are worried about the background and qualifications of the sales people you are going to supply for them. In the specification, all members of the team were described as graduates. On reflection, you can see that this was an exaggeration. Some of the team did not go to university, but all have post-school qualifications. In any case, the quality of their sales skills is the most important thing. If this proves to be a real sticking point, you are prepared to guarantee you will only use graduates for the Namaste contract.

Sales Manager

You are very proud of the sales team you have built up. You know they have the reputation within the industry and, more importantly, with doctors, as being some of the best informed and most dedicated sales people. They all undergo extensive product training before they start to work as representatives. You think this question of university qualification is completely irrelevant and would resent any attempt by Namaste to undermine the reputation of your sales team.

6 Making and responding to proposals

Objectives

Communication skills encouraging responses, making counter-proposals
Culture and tactics emotional versus neutral behaviour
Language knowledge making suggestions and proposals
Negotiating practice making and responding to proposals

Communication skills

Pre-viewing

1 Once positions have been established in a negotiation, a process of making and responding to proposals usually follows. Which side (the customer or supplier) should start the process? What are the advantages of going first and second?

2 Read the Video Negotiating Context.

Video Negotiating Context

The people

Andrew Carter
is Export Sales Manager for Okus IT. He plans to support Karen in making the new proposal.

Karen Black
is a Project Manager at Okus IT. She and Andrew plan to break the deadlock over the issue of project work by making a new proposal.

Françoise Quantin
is the current IT Manager at Levien. She is looking for a solution to the problem of logging project work.

Sean Morrissey
is from Levien's Chicago office. He is not happy with the idea of logging project work. He wants Okus to come up with a better solution.

The negotiation

The meeting has got stuck on the issue of paying for project work. The Levien team feel the Level A option (all support and project work included) is too expensive; the Level B option (just support work included) is too open-ended. They want Okus to offer something in between.

▷ 3 Watch Version 1. What do you think of Sean's tactics? Is he right to be so demanding?

▷ 4 Watch Version 1 again. How does Sean make his demands? What type of response does he get?

▷ 5 Watch Version 2. Who makes the proposal this time? What kind of response does she get?

▷ 6 Watch Version 2 again, from the point where Sean has accepted that the new proposal is good in theory, but has asked for clarification. Françoise and Karen negotiate together. What approach do they use?

Post-viewing

7 Work in pairs. Following the model of Karen and Françoise, negotiate the following by making proposals and counter-proposals. You must try to reach a conclusion or decision.

  – The company is going to invest in sponsoring a major, world-class sports team. It is your responsibility to select which sport and which team.

  – One of you has to relocate to New York to help set up a project. It would be for a minimum of twelve months. You don't know much about the relocation package yet, but you have to make a decision now. Which one of you will go?

  – It has become necessary to make budget cuts. You could let go two trainees, who have completed only six months of their training, or you could economize in other ways. Decide what you are going to do.

  – You are responsible for organizing an important dinner and evening's entertainment for a very influential client whom you know does not speak a great deal of English. You also know that this client has strong religious beliefs which mean that he/she cannot eat and drink certain things. Decide what you are going to do.

Culture and tactics

1 Read the text. Then think about your own negotiating style. Is it neutral or emotional?

> In the bad versions of this unit and some of the other units, Sean succeeds in getting an *emotional** response from the Okus team – this may be a show of frustration, anger, or even sarcasm. He will regard this type of response as a sign of weakness. His negotiating style is direct and sometimes confrontational, but he himself never gets emotionally involved.
>
> In many business cultures, detached and *neutral** behaviour is expected. Sean comes from this sort of culture. The other three operate most of the time in a neutral way but, on occasions, cannot stop themselves from showing their feelings. The two women, maybe because of inexperience, or just because of their personalities, want to communicate when they are pleased or, on the other hand, frustrated or angry. Sean puts Andrew on the defensive and this explains why he tries to fight back, arguing about Rolls Royces and Fords!

2 How would you respond in the following buyer-seller negotiations? Discuss the consequences of your response with a partner. Is the customer always right?

a To your surprise, the buyer doesn't ask for any price discount.
b The seller proposes a ridiculously high price.
c The buyer demands some confidential information (e.g. profit margins).
d The buyer suggests that your production facility is out of date.
e The buyer suggests that you should lower your prices because of the poor economic situation.
f The seller suggests that your payment terms are excessively long.
g The seller agrees to negotiate with you, but not a colleague who he or she doesn't trust.
h The buyer makes you wait much longer than expected.

* see acknowledgement on page 2

Language knowledge

'Maybe we could agree a contingency sum at the start of the year to cover urgent projects.'

1 Listen to the extract from a meeting about a joint venture project. The participants are considering proposals about who should be project leader. There are three possible candidates. Indicate below who favours whom.

	CANDIDATES		
	Peter McVitie	**Andreas Bauer**	**Francesca Rossi**
SPEAKERS			
Maura			
Nigel			
Ute			

2 Listen again and write down the expressions used to make proposals and respond to them.

a Maura's proposal _____
b Nigel's response _____
c Nigel's proposal _____
d Ute's proposal _____
e Maura's response _____
f Ute's reinforced proposal _____

Language focus Making suggestions and proposals

Making proposals

Formal
I propose ...
I suggest ...
I advise you to ...

Less formal
I think we should ...
Why don't we ...?
How/What about ...?

Responding positively

Good idea.
That sounds fine.
I go along with that.

Neutrally

That's true, but ...
I see what you're saying.
I understand why you think so.
We could do that.

Negatively

(I'm afraid) that's not possible.
We can't do that.
That is/would be out of the question.
I can't agree to that.

3 Listen to the proposals. Respond as indicated below.

a (negative) _____

b (neutral) _____

c (positive) _____

d (neutral) _____

e (positive) _____

f (negative) _____

4 Make proposals about the following.

a A five per cent cut in the training budget.

_____

b A two per cent rise in productivity.

_____

c A meal with your colleagues after work.

_____

d A company excursion to a theme park.

_____

e To reduce advertising costs.

_____

f To extend the working hours by two and a half hours per week.

_____

5 Speaking practice

Work in pairs. Practise making and responding to proposals in these situations. Follow the pattern given below.

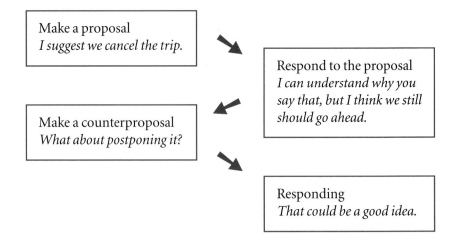

a You urgently need to employ three more people but your offices are already overcrowded.

b The company telephone bill has doubled. All managers have access to the Internet.

c Your competitors are about to launch a rival to one of your best-selling product lines.

d You are several days behind with a big order to an important customer.

e A large sum of money (about a million dollars) has been made available to spend on improving your office buildings. You have to present an action plan for how it is to be spent quickly, or you risk losing the money.

Negotiating practice

Group work (groups of 4)

In this negotiation, there are four roles. Each participant has a proposal to make and opinions about their colleagues' proposals. The objective is to try to reach a compromise decision.

The situation

The local council in your community has given permission to a building firm to construct some new houses on the edge of the town. The site is part of a park which attracts wildlife and is a popular area for recreation. Two of you represent the local community and have asked for a meeting with local council representatives.

Community representatives

Your objective is to get assurances that minimum environmental damage will be done to the park, the houses will be tastefully landscaped, and they will not spread beyond agreed limits.

Community representative 1

Your proposal is that the council should make the building company take account of the wishes of the community. You want the details of the housing development to be passed to your committee for their approval.

Community representative 2

Your proposal is that the building company should be required to plant trees around the housing estate to form a barrier between the houses and the park.

The council

Your objective is to pacify the local community. Planning permission has already been given to the builders. The community needs more housing, as many young people cannot find anywhere to live. You will see the final plans for the development of the estate, but you would not expect to show them to the community representatives.

Council representative 1

Your proposal is that you will guarantee that no more houses will be built on this land: in other words, the agreed limits of this development will be kept to and not extended.

Council representative 2

Your proposal is that the builders will have to build a high fence between the estate and the park.

Pair work

In this negotiation, you will exchange proposals and counter-proposals with your partner.

The situation

You are negotiating about cuts to your departmental staff. The negotiation is between the Head of Department and the Staff Representative.

Head of Department

You have to reduce the headcount by two. You have selected one middle manager – Kurt Steiner – for early retirement. He is fifty-four years old and is in charge of health and safety. This function will be subcontracted to an outside firm. The other person selected is Suzanna Mendez. She only joined the company fourteen months ago as a graduate trainee. She is twenty-two years old and works as a Production Planner. Her function is not essential, and you feel she stands a good chance of getting a job elsewhere.
You are not in favour of job-sharing, as you think it leads to inefficiency. You also want to keep overtime payments as this is a flexible way of dealing with peaks in demand.

Staff Representative

The staff are very unhappy about any job cuts. They know that Kurt Steiner and Suzanna Mendez have been selected and feel the choice is very unfair. You would like to propose alternative ways of reducing the monthly payroll. Two or three members of staff are prepared to consider a job-share, thus reducing the salary bill by one full-time member of staff. You also feel that overtime could be cut down by rationalizing the production schedule.

7 Bargaining

Objectives

Communication skills	maintaining positive communication
Culture and tactics	high-context versus low-context cultures
Language knowledge	exerting pressure and making conditions
Negotiating practice	bargaining practice

Communication skills

Pre-viewing

1   What can cause negotiations to fail? How important is it to maintain a positive tone throughout the meeting?

2   Read the Video Negotiating Context.

Video Negotiating Context

The people

Andrew Carter
is Export Sales Manager for Okus IT. He is beginning to feel that his team are conceding too much.

Karen Black
is a Project Manager at Okus IT. She had originally proposed to hire just two members of the Levien IT team.

Françoise Quantin
is the current IT Manager at Levien. She is very preoccupied with saving the jobs of as many of her IT team as possible.

Sean Morrissey
is from Levien's Chicago office. He does not want to have any difficulties with the Works Council (a body which represents the interests of employees).

The negotiation

The meeting returns to the issue of staffing. In their written proposal, Okus have offered to employ just two members of the Levien team – one as IT Manager, and the other as a support engineer. Any additional work, such as special projects, they plan to service from the UK, sending out project engineers from their Swindon base.

Viewing

▶ 3 Watch Version 1. How could Karen and Andrew stop the negotiation from becoming so polarized?

▶ 4 Watch Version 1 again. How do Andew and Karen try to resist the pressure from Levien?

▶ 5 Watch Version 2. How does Karen maintain positive communication this time?

▶ 6 Watch Version 2 again. When does Karen introduce the concession of taking on a third member of the team? What impact does it have?

Post-viewing

7 **Group work** (groups of 3)
Negotiate a solution to the problem in the following situation. Try to maintain positive communication, and to resolve the conflict of interests.

Student A

Your job is to monitor part of the production process in a chemical plant. On each shift there is always someone at the control panel, checking safety levels. Your daughter has a hospital appointment tomorrow afternoon. You asked your boss two weeks ago if you could leave work at lunchtime. You have just been told that you cannot leave work because the other controller is not going to be present.

Student B

Your job is to monitor part of the production process in a chemical plant. On each shift there is always someone at the control panel, checking safety levels. Yesterday you heard that you had got an interview for a new job. The first interview is tomorrow afternoon. Your boss agreed to let you go.

Student C

You are the head of the production coordination centre of a chemical plant. You forgot that you had already given permission for one of your controllers to take time off tomorrow afternoon. When the other controller asked for permission because of his/her interview, you assumed that would not cause a problem. You have called for a meeting with the two of them to sort out a solution.

I KNEW YOU WOULD BE ANGRY WITH MY PROPOSALS WHEN I AGREED TO COME HERE TODAY, BUT WE'RE WILLING TO NEGOTIATE.

Culture and tactics

High-context and low-context cultures

In a *high-context* culture, people understand a lot from the context. In other words, specific criticisms or problems are not spoken about. If you are accustomed to this sort of culture, you can understand the message from the context, rather than from what is said. Another way of putting this is to say that the message is implicit, rather than explicit. In a high-context culture it is important to avoid any negativity. Harmony is maintained by smiling and even saying 'yes' to something which you disagree with. Real sticking points in a negotiation are unlikely to be dealt with in public. It is more likely that a concession will be offered in private. In this way, harmony is maintained and there is also no loss of face.

In a *low-context* culture, people are far more explicit. Nothing is left to chance. The risk of miscomprehension is too great. Everything must be written down and clarified and, if possible, reinforced by a legal contract. Tolerance of negativity is therefore higher. People would prefer to say 'no' rather than run the risk of being misunderstood. When these two cultures come into contact with each other in a tough negotiation, the western low-context model often dominates. However, westerners need to be sensitive to the approach that will dominate when doing business in a high-context culture.

In the Okus/Levien negotiation, Sean typifies a low-context approach. In the first version of the bargaining session over staff, Andrew also follows this model. Karen tries to reduce the negativity. In the good version, harmony is maintained partly by Karen's positive communication, but also because she and Andrew have a concession up their sleeve.

What would you say in the following situations?

a You have been waiting a long time to be served in a shop. Finally it is your turn and another customer suddenly pushes in front of you.

b You have been negotiating for several weeks for a training contract abroad. You have spent a lot of time and money in specifying the training. You have discovered that the client has just signed a contract with a competitor, and is using your specification.

c You have just negotiated a very profitable annual contract for a fixed quantity of your product to be delivered monthly at an agreed price. Following the first month's delivery, you receive a fax indicating that they will require fewer products during the second month.

Language knowledge

'Labour laws here are real tough and we probably won't be able to sign this contract if we don't get a better offer.'

1 Listen to the extracts. In each case a concession is offered but there is a condition attached. Complete the table.

Extract	concession	condition
one		
two		
three		
four		

2 Listen again and complete the conditional offers.
   a **Extract one** If you could offer us an annual contract ...we _____ _____ one per cent.

   b **Extract two** ... we've got the contract if we _____ _____ money?

   c **Extract three** If you were late paying, we _____ _____ payment.

   d **Extract four** If they came up with a better offer, we _____ _____ match it.

HIS EXCELLENCY WILL AGREE TO YOUR PROPOSAL IF YOU THROW IN YOUR WATCH.

Language focus Exerting pressure and making conditions

Exerting pressure

If you can't ..., we'll have to look elsewhere.
I'm afraid we'll have to call it a day unless ...

Making concessions

We could offer you ...
We might consider ...
What would you say if we offered you ...?
We might be able to ...

Attaching conditions

But we would want ...
... as long as ...
... on one condition ...
... provided that ...

Grammar point

Standard conditional sentence (threatening/asserting pressure)
We will have to cancel if you don't offer us something better.
We won't be doing business with you unless we get a substantial discount.

Standard hypothetical conditional sentence
We would offer you one per cent if you guaranteed payment within thirty days.
We couldn't guarantee payment unless you promised a firm discount.

---

3   Use the conditional constructions above (*if ...* or *unless ...*) to exert pressure in the following situations.

For example:
(supplier to company) Sign the contract immediately/get a discount.
Unless you sign the contract immediately, you won't get a discount.

a   (company to IT providers) Cancel the contract/reduce your fees.
b   (factory to supplier) Choose another supplier/better offer.
c   (negotiator to negotiator) End the negotiation/a concession.
d   (boss to employee) Lose your job/improve performance.
e   (employee to boss) Leave the company/better salary.
f   (headhunted job candidate to boss) Accept a new job/bigger office.

4   Using the ideas below, make offers and attach conditions.
For example:
offer: extend the contract   condition: a one per cent discount
We could extend your contract as long as you offered us a one per cent discount.

	offers	conditions
a	two per cent discount	guaranteed orders
b	a firm order	early delivery
c	a new car	reach sales targets
d	a position on the board	agree to work overseas
e	a new office	work this weekend
f	a salary rise	move to Liverpool

5　Complete the dialogue using appropriate words and expressions from the *Language focus* section.

A: We seem to have reached a stalemate. We're not going to progress _____ you can make us a better offer.
B: We might be able to offer something better but _____.
A: What's that?
B: You would have to guarantee us a fixed order every month for a year.
A: We might be able to do that, _____ we feel you are the right supplier for us.
B: OK. If you _____ give us this guarantee, we _____ be prepared to reduce our prices by fifteen per cent.

6　**Speaking practice**

Work in pairs. Script a similar dialogue to the one above for the following situation.

A supplier and a customer are negotiating about transport costs. The supplier is willing to include them in the price of the contract, if the customer agrees to his payment terms. The customer will agree to better payment terms so long as delivery times are guaranteed.

The supplier should start off the negotiation like this:
supplier: *We might consider including them in the contract, but ...*

7　Read the following text about a recent big business deal. Then replace each word in italics with the word or expression below which is nearest in meaning.

David and Goliath battle it out

Analysts were shocked by news that Unica PLC, a relative newcomer in consumer electronics, has made an offer to take over Amamoto Electronics. Insiders are saying that Unica's [1] *bid* at least [2] *matches* their main competitor, Fisor, in this takeover battle. Amamoto's value has been [3] *quoted* around the 2.5 billion mark. If Unica is to [4] *beat* Fisor, it will have to [5] *outbid* this by quite a hefty [6] *margin*. They can expect some board-room [7] *haggling* over the next week but clearly believe Amamoto will have to [8] *give in* to shareholder pressure to accept their generous offer. Share prices of all three companies have been pushed upwards by constant speculation.

a equals　　b bargaining　　c defeat　　d surrender
e offer　　f exceed　　g estimated　　h amount

8   Use the right form of the terms from exercise 7 to complete the sentences below.

   a   We asked the supplier to put in a new _____. They did, and it not only _____ other_____ we had received, it actually _____ them.

   b   I don't enjoy _____. I always get knocked down on price and end up _____ to the seller.

   c   Unfortunately we lost the contract. One of the competitors _____ us by a considerable _____.

   d   We_____ them what we believed was a fair price, but they are not happy. They are going to want to _____.

Negotiating practice

Pair work

The situation

A small company wants to have its computer network maintained and serviced. It has entered a negotiation with an IT service provider. The negotiation has reached the bargaining phase where the critical issues of prices and type of service need to be resolved. One of you is the supplier, the other the customer. Prepare your position and then bargain with your partner to achieve a satisfactory result.

The supplier

You want to negotiate for an annual contract to service all computer equipment at your customer's premises. For this you want to charge ten per cent of current value of the equipment (calculated at £125,000). For this price you offer one annual maintenance visit plus a twenty-four-hour call-out service to deal with any failures or breakdowns, 365 days a year. To get the contract, you are willing to reduce the fee from ten per cent to a bottom line of eight per cent. If you reduce the fee, you will want to extend the contract over two years.

The customer

You need a company to maintain and service your computer network. You find their proposed fee of ten per cent of current hardware value very high. They have estimated your computer hardware to be worth £125,000. You have had an independent estimate which values it at £90,000. You would be willing to pay £9,000 a year, as long as the call-out is always the same day as a fault is reported.

Group work (groups of 4)

The situation

A training provider is negotiating with a large company for the provision of management and sales training for the next year. The client company wants the training organization to reduce its prices in line with the quantity of training. Two of you are suppliers from the training company, the other two are from the client company. Prepare your positions and then negotiate to achieve a satisfactory result for both sides.

The suppliers (2)

You need to prepare the following position:
- You have offered a variety of training courses. If all go ahead you will be doing one hundred training days for this client.
- Your prices have been calculated on type of training – as a guideline: management training is charged at a rate of £600 per day, and sales training is £500 per day.
- You do not normally offer discounts as there are no cost savings in quantity. Each course has to be specially prepared.
- You are willing to make the following concessions if necessary: a ten per cent discount if a hundred training days is reached, or a five per cent discount if eighty days is reached.

The customers (2)

You need to prepare the following position:
- You are offering this company a lot of training. You want significant price discounts.
- You are not prepared to guarantee any number of days training as it can be cancelled at short notice.
- You feel their daily rates could be cut by £100 per day.
- If they do this, you are willing to pay within fifteen days of a course taking place.

8 Conclusion and agreement

Objectives

Communication skills	**summarizing and agreeing follow-up**
Culture and tactics	**win-win versus win-lose**
Language knowledge	**concluding and closing**
Negotiating practice	**closing the negotiation**

Communication skills

Pre-viewing

1 What should happen at the end of a negotiation? What issues do you need to agree on before closing the meeting?

2 Read the Video Negotiating Context.

Video Negotiating Context

The people

Andrew Carter
is Export Sales Manager for Okus IT. He is keen to get home, having achieved some sort of agreement.

Karen Black
is a Project Manager at Okus IT. She feels there are still some issues which need discussion.

Françoise Quantin
is the current IT Manager at Levien. She has a dinner engagement and having achieved most of their objectives, wants to end the meetings quickly.

Sean Morrissey
is from Levien's Chicago office. He feels Levien have got a good deal. As far as he is concerned, there are just loose ends to be tied up by Karen and Françoise at a later date.

The negotiation

They have reached agreement about staffing and the level of support. There remain some questions about which staff are to be hired and also the contingency sum, which will be used to fund special projects. Karen would also like to clarify the payment terms.

Viewing

▶ 3 Watch Version 1. What should Françoise have done in this final session?

▶ 4 Watch Version 1 again. Why is Karen so angry with Andrew? Why do you think Andrew is so happy to leave?

▶ 5 Watch Version 2. How does Françoise handle the closing session?

▶ 6 Watch Version 2 again. Françoise is businesslike and polite in making her apologies for leaving so quickly. Pick out these moments:
- she summarizes
- she agrees action
- she apologizes for leaving quickly.

Post-viewing

7 What steps do you go through to close a negotiation effectively? Use the three headings below to help you draw up a detailed checklist for closing a negotiation. When you have finished, compare yours with the one in the Answer Key on page 81.
- Summarizing
- Follow-up action
- Departing

Culture and tactics

1 Work in pairs. Each of you should read one of the texts below. Prepare to present a summary of the text in your own words to your partner.

The win-lose philosophy

In Version 1 of Unit 8 Sean concludes: 'It's been a very productive day – a definite result'.

Levien have got what Sean wanted. Okus have agreed to take on four members of staff – two more than they wanted. They have also been pushed into offering an alternative level of support – one which they may find hard to service. Karen is trying hard to compensate for her 'defeat' by keeping them talking about payment and contingency sums. Andrew wants to 'cut his losses' and run! Karen is left with a sense of disappointment and failure.

The win-win philosophy

In Version 2, Françoise ends on a different note: 'Goodbye then. I hope we both got the deal we wanted.' And Karen replies: 'I think we did.'

Okus have agreed to take on three members of staff and they have conceded on the support contract. But a positive, collaborative approach has dominated throughout. Françoise's philosophy has won the day: 'I will have to work with these people and I want a positive relationship'.

A cultural clash occurs when these two negotiating philosophies meet. The win-lose approach treats the negotiation as an end in itself, forgetting that it only serves as the starting point for a longer-term relationship between supplier and customer.

---

2 Discuss the following tactics. Which do you agree with and why? What other advice would you give?

a ● Never negotiate a single issue.

b ● Always bargain from a position of strength.

c ● Don't let your negotiating partners feel too comfortable.

d ● Identify and reinforce the weak points in their argument.

e ● Never show your real feelings.

f ● Keep your strongest cards up your sleeves.

Language knowledge

'So, we have agreed an initial one-year contract on the basis of full support and minimal project work. We will meet again here to ...'

1 Listen to the closing stages of four negotiations. Tick (✓) the stages they go through.

Extract	one	two	three	four
a Summary of points of agreement/ disagreement				
b Follow-up action e.g. minutes of the meeting, further contacts				
c positive ending				

2 Listen again and identify the expressions used to:
a indicate the end of the meeting:

Extract one   _____

Extract two   _____

b introduce a summary:

Extract one   _____

Extract two   _____

Extract three   _____

Extract four   _____

c talk about follow-up action:

Extract one _____

Extract two _____

Extract three _____

Extract four _____

d end on a positive note:

Extract one _____

Extract two _____

Extract three _____

Extract four _____

Language focus Concluding and closing

Closing signal

More formal
That brings us to the end of ...
I think we have covered everything.

Less formal
I think we can call it a day.
I think that covers it.
Let's stop there.

Progress made

We've taken a major step forward.
We've made excellent/good/some progress.
We've taken a step in the right direction.
We didn't get as far as we hoped, but ...

Summarizing

Let's go over the main points again.
Can I just run over the main points?
We've agreed the following ...
There's still the question of ... to resolve.
Outstanding issues are ...

Subjects

On the ... front, we agreed ...
As far as ... is concerned, we agreed ...

Checking and confirming

Is that an accurate summary?
Does that reflect what we said?
Is there anything you want to add?

Follow-up documentation

Would you like that in writing?
We'll put together a written proposal.
We'll let you have a detailed summary.
Can you draft that before the next meeting?

Next meeting

I suggest we meet on/at ...
Could you manage ...?
Shall we say four o'clock?

Closing

I'm sure we would all agree that we have had a successful meeting.
It remains for me to thank you for coming and ...

3 Complete the sentences with the appropriate words and expressions from the *Language focus* section.

a Let me just _____ _____ the main points.

b I think that just about _____ it.

c It _____ _____ _____ _____ say how much we appreciate your contribution.

d Does that accurately _____ what we agreed during the meeting?

e Could you _____ a written proposal before the next meeting?

f I _____ we meet later in the week. Would that suit you?

g As _____ _____ payment _____ _____, there are still some _____ issues to resolve.

h I'm afraid we didn't _____ _____ _____ as we hoped.

i Let's _____ _____ _____ day.

4 a At the end of a negotiation we often make a remark about the meeting. For example:
That was a very positive start. I look forward to our next meeting.
Find the positive adjectives we use to talk about meetings and negotiations from these nouns.

For example:
product – *productive* (*The meeting was extremely productive.*)

a fruit _____

b help _____

c use _____

d information _____

e stimulant _____

f interest _____

b To further intensify these adjectives, we use words like:

extremely	*really*	*very*

For example:
That was really useful.

Now listen to the remarks on the tape and respond with a positive comment on the meeting. In each case, combine a modifier and an adjective.

a _____

b _____

c _____

d _____

e _____

f _____

5   Complete this script from the end of a negotiation using words from the box below.

> *agreed brings suggest resolve add run over say fruitful*
> *outstanding left committed summary resolve issues OK*

A: So that _____ us to the end of a very _____ negotiation. It's been a pleasure to work with you today. Let me just _____ the areas of agreement and also highlight one or two _____ issues which we still need to _____. Firstly, we have _____ a quota of 160,000 units per month. Secondly, we have _____ ourselves to processing at least 150,000 every four weeks. Thirdly, and just as important, we will manage the stock much more actively. Is that an accurate _____?

B: That's fine. I just wanted to _____ that we think the 160,000 is a conservative figure.

A: You may well be right. Let's review it again in six months. There were two _____ which have been _____ open. There's the question of rejects and how we handle them and there is also the more difficult problem of payment. I _____ we meet again next week to try to _____ these issues. Would that be _____?

B: Fine. Shall we _____ next Thursday at, um, ten o'clock?

A: Fine. See you then.

6   **Speaking practice**

You have reached the end of the first stage of a negotiation about the supply of electronic components. The meeting has been successful, and you have managed to agree about a number of important issues. Work in pairs, taking it in turns to chair the meeting and close this stage of the negotiation.

Student A

You are chairing the meeting. Go through the following stages to bring the negotiation to a close. Make sure Student B answers any questions you may ask. When you have finished, change roles.

a Suggest you end the meeting.
b Ask if he/she would like a summary.
c Introduce three subjects for summary.
d Mention one or two issues not yet agreed.
e Check summary is OK.
f Comment on progress made.
g Suggest another meeting.
h End on a positive note.

Student B

Student A is chairing the meeting and is now bringing your negotiations to a close, following through the different stages above. Listen and respond to any questions Student A asks you. When you have finished, change roles.

Negotiating practice

Group work (groups of 4)

The task below involves three short negotiations. Carry out the negotiations. Make sure you close the meetings effectively.

Student A

You are the Sales Manager for Shigoru International. You are planning to run a sales conference at a hotel. You have invited three possible hotels to come and discuss the offers they have made. Your objective is to decide which hotel to choose (the best value for money). Read the requirements below and then prepare for each meeting by reading through the offer the hotel has made.

Requirements

Conference rooms	plenary room – to hold forty delegates
	syndicate rooms – three, to hold ten per room
Accommodation	forty double rooms
Full board service	breakfast, lunch, and evening meal
	(plus coffee breaks)
Facilities	leisure facilities would be an advantage
Dates and duration	two days (two nights) in March: over a weekend
Budget	delegate rate (to include all above costs): £100 – £120 per person per night
	total budget: max. £10,000.

Student B

You are in charge of conferences at the Park Hotel. Following a phone call, you have prepared the following quote. In order to get the business, you may be willing to reduce your prices slightly.

Park Hotel

Dear Sir,

Please find below our preliminary offer in response to your request. As stated on the phone, we would be willing to negotiate the final package and look forward to meeting you on Monday 4th February at 14.00.

Client	*Shigoru International*
Conference dates	Saturday 14th and Sunday 15th March
Delegates	approx. forty
Facilities reserved	plenary room, plus three syndicate rooms
	full audio-visual support
	forty double rooms with bathroom
	Saturday: breakfast, lunch, and dinner
	Sunday: breakfast, lunch
	free use of leisure club (swimming pool, sauna, jacuzzi)
Delegate rate	£125 per person per night

Student C

You are the owner of the Hotel Grand. You could just accommodate Shigoru International for a conference in March. You are trying to break into the conference market and are willing to negotiate on price to get the business.

```
Dear Ms Morrow

It was a pleasure to talk to you on the phone yesterday.
Below you will find our offer for your planned sales conference
in March.
We look forward to discussing it further next week.

Conference specification for: Shigoru International.

Dates                     Saturday 14th and Sunday 15th March
                          (arr. Friday evening?)
Delegates                 approx. forty
Facilities reserved       plenary room, plus three syndicate rooms
                          thirty double rooms with bathroom,
                          ten single rooms (shared facilities)
                          Saturday: breakfast, lunch, and dinner
                          Sunday: breakfast, lunch
                          tennis and golf in the grounds
Delegate rate             £98 per person per night
```

Student D

You are the Manager of Hotel Maxim. Forty delegates is more than you could normally take. However, you are converting an annexe to the hotel and this will be ready by March. The conference rooms are comfortable and attractive, but will be a bit small for such a large group. On the other hand, you can assure Shigoru of a very warm welcome and excellent service.

Hotel **Maxim**

Dear Sirs,

We have great pleasure in sending you the following offer and look forward to our meeting next week.

Conference details

Dates	Saturday 14th and Sunday 15th March
Delegates	approx. forty
Facilities reserved	board room, plus three meeting rooms
	twenty-five double rooms with bathroom
	in main hotel, fifteen in annexe
	Saturday: breakfast, lunch, and dinner
	Sunday: breakfast, lunch
	billiard table, games room
Delegate rate	£88 per person per night

Answer Key

Unit 1

Communication skills

1 A negotiation is a meeting or a series of meetings in which the parties need each other's agreement to reach a specific objective.

2 It is important to discuss strategies beforehand and to decide on the approach your team is going to take. Members of the team need to be clear about the objectives of the negotiation and what role they are expected to play in achieving those objectives.

4 There are a number of indications that the negotiation will not go well:
  – Karen and Andrew do not communicate as a team.
  – Karen and Andrew have different agendas.
  – Sean and Andrew get off to a bad start.
  – Andrew forgets to introduce Karen.
  – Sean and Andrew separate from Karen and Françoise.

5 It is clear that they haven't discussed their strategy, approach, or roles. Karen is talking about their strategy, Andrew is thinking about personalities. Both these areas should have been discussed beforehand.

6 If both teams were properly prepared, Françoise and Sean would have handled the introductions much better. Françoise, as the host, should be in charge of these introductions. She needs to make sure the Okus team is properly welcomed and made to feel at ease.

7 Karen and Andrew are seen to work as a team. They know how they are going to approach the negotiation. The welcome involves everybody and sets the tone for the meeting to follow. Françoise establishes the fact that she wants to take time getting to know the Okus team.

8 Françoise greets Karen and then let's Sean introduce Andrew. In this way all four are involved. Françoise makes sure time is given to some small talk. Andrew and Sean re-establish their contact.

9 Negotiation checklist
  Objectives
  – What's the best we can get?
  – What's the worst we can get?
  – What is our bottom line?

Strategies
- What are the main areas of negotiation?
- What are likely to be sticking points?
- What is the best order to discuss these points?
- What concessions can we give to achieve our main aim?

Roles
- Who is responsible for different stages of the negotiation?
- What special skills/knowledge do individual members of the team have?
- What do we know about the other team?

Communication
- How are we going to maintain positive communication?
- Who is taking notes or minutes?
- Who is going to ask questions?

Language knowledge

1   a Extract three
    b Extract two
    c Extract one
    d Extract four

2   a CHAIRMAN: *On behalf of Unica I'm very glad to welcome you to …*
    b PETER: *Hello, everyone. My name's Peter Snelson. I'm the Corporate Affairs Director here in the UK, and I'll be in charge of producing the press statements …*
    c ULRIKE: *Hello. I'm Ulrike Kristofferson, in charge of Strategic Marketing …*
    d YVES (1): *This is Luca Gardini. He looks after our offices in Southern Europe.*
    e YVES (2): *And I think everyone knows Gabriella?*

3   Extract two: *And that was actually one of the things I wanted to discuss with you this morning.*
    Extract three: *So, how's business in your sector?*
    Extract four: *Sorry to interrupt, but I think we'd better get started now.*

4   Here are some suggestions. Other responses are possible.
    a On behalf of …, I'm very glad to welcome you to … or, Welcome to … Thank you for coming all this way.
    b Hello … Good/Nice to see you again.
    c Let me introduce you to … She's responsible for …
    d How do you do?/Nice to meet you. This is … He's in charge of …
    e How was your journey/flight? Is this your first visit to …? Is your hotel comfortable?
    f Would you like some coffee? Would you like anything to drink?
    g We're short of time, so perhaps we'd better get started.

5   Here are some suggestions. Other responses are possible.
    a *Well, I'm delighted to welcome you all to our processing plant here in Gdansk.*
    It's nice to be here.
    b *Let me introduce you to Mehmet Tarkan. He's our key Account Manager.*
    (How do you do?) Nice to meet you. I'm …

   c *How was the weather when you left home?*
     Pretty awful. It's much better here.
   d *How was the flight over?*
     Fine. No problems.
   e *Is everything OK with the hotel?*
     It seems very comfortable, thank you.
   f *Right. Let's get started then.*
     Good idea.

6 a iii   b vi   c i   d vii   e v   f ii   g iv

7 a It's difficult to predict what's going to happen. I think we should just *play it by ear*.
   b We've really got *bogged down* in detail and lost sight of our overall objectives.
   c We could end up losing money on the contract if we are not careful. The chief negotiator on the other team is very experienced and always *drives a hard bargain*.
   d Our margins are very tight. There's very little *room to manoeuvre*.
   e I know they think we are charging too much, but if they try to *knock us down* on price, we're going to have to insist on better payment terms.
   f They are very persuasive negotiators and will throw a lot of impressive-sounding figures at you, so you should *be on your guard*.
   g Ideally the new buildings will be nearer the airport, but if that proves too expensive, or there is nothing available, our *fall-back position* is to site the factory here.

Unit 2

Communication skills

1 Informal negotiations don't need an agenda. In some cases, you are negotiating just one point. An agenda is often best negotiated rather than imposed at the start of a meeting. Usually the host company should be responsible for chairing/controlling the negotiation.

3 Karen and Andrew expect the negotiation to be structured and they assume there will be an opportunity to present their package. Françoise jumps in at the deep end by introducing her main preoccupation – staffing levels.

4 Most negotiators start by identifying the common ground. In other words, the points which both sides agree on. Then you have a firm basis to discuss problem areas. It is important that the Okus team do not show too strong an emotional response to Sean's aggression. Sean will see this as a weakness.

5 Françoise keeps total control over the opening phase. She has clearly prepared well and knows where she is going.

6 Françoise's steps:
   – clarification of the position of Okus versus the competition
   – statement of objectives
   – introduction of agenda
   – check on roles
   – check on timing/end of day.

7   Negotiation checklist
    a Introductions/roles   Who is present?
                                 What roles do the participants have in
                                 the negotiation?
    b Purpose/objectives   What are the shared expectations?
                                 What are the critical issues?
    c Agenda/structure   How are we going to start and finish?
    d Timing (including breaks) How long do we have?
                                 What are the arrangements for
                                 breaks/meals?
    e Procedure/process   Are we going to chair this negotiation?
                                 Will there be presentations/question-and-
                                 answer sessions?
                                 Are we going to take minutes?

Culture and tactics

2 a universalist
   b particularist
   c universalist
   d universalist

Language knowledge

1

Extract	introduction	objectives	agenda	timing	roles	procedures
one			✓	✓	✓	
two			✓	✓		
three	✓	✓	✓			
four		✓	✓	✓		
five				✓	✓	✓
six				✓		✓

2 a The penalty issue is on the agenda in the morning. Payment terms are on
      the agenda for the afternoon.
   b Pricing is the first issue to be discussed.
   c The market has become more competitive and their combined strength
      will give both parties advantages, not least in terms of the dealer
      network.
   d The delivery contract will be changed from a monthly to an annual basis.
   e Contentious issues are on the agenda for after lunch.
   f Today's meeting will last until three/most of the day.

3 a Can we just *go* through the agenda?
   b It won't *take* more than a couple of minutes.
   c It would be easier if we *took* the question of staff first.
   d Don't worry. John will *take* the minutes.
   e Françoise is going to *give* a brief presentation.
   f Then we can *go* round the table.
   g We'll *come* to that in a moment.
   h I think we should *put* that last.
   i So, that *gives* us just half an hour.

5 a pros   and *cons*
     advantages and disadvantages
     strengths   and *weaknesses*
     pluses   and minuses

6 a iv b vii c i d ix e vi f ii g iii h v i viii

7 a We have *lost ground* to our competitors.
   b We've *covered a lot of ground.*
   c Their offer *cut the ground from under us.*
   d Don't give in. *Hold your ground.*
   e We need to *find some common ground.*
   f We're just *going over the same ground.*
   g You must *keep both feet on the ground.*
   h You're *on dangerous ground.*

Unit 3

Communication skills

1 It's important to give yourself some room to manoeuvre later. Therefore you shouldn't present your best offer immediately.

2 Simply ask for it. Make sure when you are presenting that you check frequently that the audience is following and has an opportunity to ask questions and comment.

4 He hides behind his slides. He doesn't make contact with his audience. He doesn't address their needs. He is inflexible and finds it difficult to adapt. Above all, he doesn't develop two-way communication.

5 He needs to identify the critical issues for Levien and address them. He then needs to make sure he is going down the right road, by checking and encouraging participation.

6 His style is now inclusive. He involves Levien in the presentation. He makes good contact with his audience.

7 He encourages interruptions and questions. Andrew and Karen work as a team. He shows he is in control, but flexible enough to change direction.

Culture and tactics

1 Here are some suggestions. Other responses are possible.
   a How much do you charge?
   b That's too expensive.
   c We need a good offer on delivery.
   d Who do you report to? *or* Who's your boss?
   e Marketing is absolutely critical.

2 Here are some suggestions. Other responses are possible.
   a I'm not entirely convinced by these forecasts.
   b We'd like to know something about your planning.
   c I'd be interested to hear a bit about payment.
   d Your costs could cause one or two problems.
   e Perhaps we could talk a little bit about figures.

Language knowledge

1

Extract	talking at	talking with
one	✓	
two		✓
three		✓
four	✓	

2

Extract	one	two	three	four
inviting to interrupt		✓		
negotiating agenda		✓	✓	
considering what they already know		✓	✓	
checking for agreement		✓	✓	
use of we/let's			✓	

3 Here are some suggestions. Other responses are possible.
  a Could we finish at five – if that's all right with you?
  b I hope you don't mind if Miss Higa sits in during the negotiation?
  c Perhaps we could take a break now. Is that OK?
  d Could we look at these three areas this morning?
  e I would like to go through the written offer clause by clause, if that's OK?
  f Do you mind if I answer your questions at the end?

4 Here are some suggestions. Other responses are possible.
  a Let's start by looking at the rising production costs.
  b Wouldn't you agree that timing is essential?
  c Perhaps we should identify who our main competitors are first.
  d Shall we discuss transport issues at the end?
  e We think the main problem is the computer system. Would you agree?

Unit 4

Communication skills

1 Some advantages of listening well:
  – You understand the other party's negotiating position.
  – You develop arguments that respond to their needs.
  – You demonstrate that you are sympathetic to their position.
  – You show that you respect and value what they have to say.

What might stop you from listening:
  – You are thinking about what you are going to say.
  – You have decided that the speaker is not worth listening to.
  – You have decided that you know what the speaker is going to say.
  – You have decided that you disagree with the speaker.

2a Techniques for effective listening include:
  – Keeping an open mind.
  – Clarifying what you do not understand – by asking questions if necessary.

b Techniques for ensuring others listen include:
- – Checking for comprehension.
- – Pausing to give people time to ask questions.
- – Allowing comments and questions.

4 She is unable to achieve her objective – clarifying the contract pricing – because of frequent and unstructured interruptions. Sean and Françoise are not listening to her. She can't keep the meeting on track.

5 She needs to be more assertive in handling the interruptions. She should keep her objective in mind while maintaining a positive tone.

6 Françoise listens actively. She shows that she understands and interprets Karen's explanation. She helps the communication to be successful.

7 Karen takes command when Sean asks a question she is not ready for. In this way she achieves her objective of clarifying the pricing structure. Andrew and Karen work as a team, which further supports the positive communication.

Language knowledge

1

Extract	listen well	listen badly
one		✓
two	✓	
three		✓
four	✓	

2

Extract	one	two	three	four
opportunity to ask questions	✓	✓	✓	✓
questions on the subject		✓		✓
questions off the subject	✓		✓	
opportunity to answer question		✓		✓
no opportunity to answer question	✓		✓	
check answer is satisfactory		✓		
encourage/show interest		✓		✓

3 Here are some suggestions. Other responses are possible.
- **a** *I think one of the critical questions is staff levels.*
  Could you tell me something about the staffing?
- **b** *There are two things we need to look at; firstly, maintenance, and secondly, safety.*
  I'd be interested to start with the question of maintenance.
- **c** *As you know, we have considerable experience in your field.*
  Could tell me more about your experience?
- **d** *We have concentrated over the last few months on improving standards.*
  I'd be interested to know how your standards have improved.

e *Our biggest challenge in the coming year will be coping with the new environmental legislation, and the effect this will have on our production processes.*
Could you tell us something about this new legislation?

4 Here are some suggestions. Other responses are possible.
a *Our sales have responded to the changes in market conditions, and we have reached a high point this month.*
Could you be more specific about the sales figures?
b *We've got the best person for the job, so we don't have to look any further.*
Could you tell me exactly why she is the best person?
c *We've sent out a lot of invitations, so we expect large numbers to attend.*
Could you tell me exactly how many invitations you sent out?
d *The costs have come down, so we are able to offer much more competitive prices.*
Could you be more specific about the costs?
e *We have already spent much too long on this project.*
Could you tell me exactly how much time has been spent on it?

5 Here are some suggestions. Other responses are possible.
a So you think it's got to be a man?
b So your prices are going to rise?
c Does this mean you can't offer some kind of discount?
d So you think it might be a risk doing business with this company?
e So you think we should ask for some quotes from other suppliers?

6 Here are some suggestions. Other responses are possible.
a *Would you like to hear about the cost breakdown?*
I certainly would.
b *Shall we take a break for lunch?*
Good idea.
c *I've told you about the technical side of things. Shall I outline the commercial package we are offering?*
Go ahead.
d *I'll start by pointing out the pluses and minuses of the joint venture. Does that sound OK?*
Yes, that sounds fine.
e *And when you're ready, I'll just finish with a brief summary of our development plans for next year.*
Fine. Go ahead.

8 a The consultant's *fees* are astronomical!
b Could you give me a *ballpark figure* for the conversion?
c When will you be *invoicing* us?
d Your hourly *rate* seems to be above the industry average.
e How much do you *charge* per day?
f If you book well in advance, you get a *discount*.
g The problem is too many people are taking a *commission* on the final price.

9 a Can you give me a *ballpark figure* for how much you plan to charge for the hardware?
 b Do you get any *commission* on the sale?
 c Can you send me the *invoice* with all the others at the end of the month?
 d How much do you *charge* per hour for support?
 e Could you give us some kind of a *discount*, considering this is such a big order?
 f I suggest that we don't use lawyers – their *fees* are too high!

Unit 5

Communication skills

1 Risks of conflict
 – personal offence
 – complete breakdown in communication
 – high levels of stress
 – negative effect on the deal.

 Potential benefits of conflict
 – move the negotiation forward quickly
 – reveals differences which need to be resolved
 – greater final understanding of positions.

4 The conflict has become personalized and Andrew has taken offence.

5 They disagree about the tactics which Sean has adopted. Sean deliberately introduced conflict in order to manipulate them. Françoise cannot understand this approach. She is concerned that she may have to work with Okus, long after Sean has returned to the States.

6 Sean makes the same points but this time avoids personalizing his anxieties. When he sees that he may cause offence, he reassures them. During the time-out, we see that Sean is still playing a tactical game but it is more thoughtful and avoids personalizing the potential conflict.

7 They use the time-out to assess their progress, rather than argue about strategy. They identify their concern and decide that they will wait for Okus to make a proposal.

Language knowledge

1
Extract	confrontational	collaborative
one	✓	
two	✓	
three		✓
four		✓

2 a If you *touch my budget*, sales *will go down.*
 b Well, I can see *we need to share the cuts across the company,* but we also *have to decide what is essential, and what is more peripheral.*
 c Sure, sure, but some *of the training you organize is hardly central.* I mean, *assertiveness training – what's that all about?*

d But I think we'd all agree *that a delay in some of the training programmes wouldn't necessarily be too critical to the business.*
There may be *one or two programmes we could put back, but I'm not sure ...*

3 Here are some suggestions. Other responses are possible.
  a We could perhaps cut the advertising budget.
  b PR expenditure may be a little bit too high.
  c You might analyse your costs in a bit more detail.
  d I'm afraid there is very little room for cuts in my budget.
  e Wouldn't we all agree that we could cut this budget?
  f Maybe you could have a look at the proposal.
  g May I suggest you take a look at page thirty-two of the document.
  h I'm afraid we were expecting a rather better offer.

4 **a** I've tasted better food.
  b Could you try to be early tomorrow?
  c I'm afraid your forecasts are not so reliable.
  d You could be a bit more experienced.
  e Your quotation is not as low as we hoped.
  f Your financial position could be more secure.

5 Here are some suggestions. Other responses are possible.
  A: I'm afraid your figures for last year don't look so good.
  B: No, they could be better.
  A: I'm not sure how we can do business on this basis.
  B: Sorry, could you explain?
  A: Well, we're worried about your track record. It could be stronger.
  B: I'm surprised you should say that. Perhaps you've forgotten some of our excellent customer references?
  A: No, I haven't forgotten. It's just that they haven't been with you for very long.
  B: I think you'll find that we have some very well-established clients. For example, we've been working with Phoenix International for five years.
  A: I'm afraid we like to see a slightly longer track record.
  B: I understand, but as I'm sure you know, we've only been in business for six years!

6 Here are some suggestions. Other responses are possible.
  A: There are rather a lot of electrical components in the warehouse at the moment. You must have over-ordered. Your department could be a bit better organized.
  B: Well, your department could be better informed. We ordered extra because we have had such problems with supply. There have been long delays waiting for orders, and the company loses money.
  A: Well, I'm afraid that the company is losing money now in storage costs. Storage is not cheap because the components are fragile and we have to keep them in special conditions. There isn't much room for other orders.
  B: There is a surplus partly because the factory has not used quite as many components as you predicted. Your predictions have been a bit inaccurate this year.

A: Well, I'm afraid that it is your department that is not very well informed. Didn't you know that a large order was cancelled, and we were forced to reduce our output?

B: I'm afraid that we didn't receive this information in time. Your department takes rather a long time to get new information to us.

A: The Purchasing Department is not all that responsive. We didn't know if you had received the message or not.

A: Perhaps we could try and think of some ways to improve communication between our departments.

Unit 6

Communication skills

1 The supplier will usually be expected to start this process. The advantage is then given to the customer who doesn't have to show his hand until he first hears what the supplier is proposing. On the other hand, making a proposal first may set the parameters for discussion and it could be an advantage if you want the negotiation to go in a certain direction.

3 He doesn't give Okus a chance to make their proposal. He pushes Okus into a corner where they have very little room to move. He also antagonizes them. He is following his win-lose philosophy of negotiation.

4 He is very direct and confrontational – he seems to be saying: 'Either you give me what I want or there's no deal'. Andrew responds first pompously and then sarcastically.

5 Karen makes the proposal. Sean responds directly but more politely. Françoise helps by making some more suggestions.

6 Karen sees a problem, then Françoise suggests a way round it. Andrew and Karen are worried about how it would work in practice. Françoise makes a proposal, Karen asks a question, and Françoise clarifies. Finally, Karen responds positively.

Language knowledge

1

	CANDIDATES		
	Peter McVitie	**Andreas Bauer**	**Francesca Rossi**
SPEAKERS			
Maura		✓	
Nigel			✓
Ute	✓		

2 a Maura's proposal: *I would like to suggest we seriously consider Andreas.*
   b Nigel's response: *I'm surprised, Maura. I thought you would go for Francesca.*
   c Nigel's proposal: *I think we should go for Francesca.*
   d Ute's proposal: *What about Peter Mcvitie?*
   e Maura's response: *That's all true, Ute, but don't you think it's time we gave Andreas a chance?*
   f Ute's reinforced proposal: *I really strongly advise you to go for Peter.*

3 Here are some suggestions. Other responses are possible.
   a *Why don't we take a break now?* I don't think that's a good idea. (negative)
   b *I propose we wait until Christmas.* Yes, we could do that. (neutral)
   c *I advise you to hire this woman.* I agree to that. (positive)
   d *I would propose that we delay the decision.* I understand why you think so. (neutral)
   e *I think we should hire the man.* That sounds fine. (positive)
   f *I want us to cancel the project.* I can't agree to that. (negative)

4 Here are some suggestions. Other responses are possible.
   a I think we should cut the training budget by five per cent.
   b I suggest we aim for a two per cent rise in productivity.
   c How about going for a meal after work?
   d Why don't we go to a theme park this year for the company excursion?
   e I advise you to reduce advertising costs.
   f I propose that we extend working hours by two and a half hours per week.

Unit 7

Communication skills

1 Negotiations can fail for a variety of reasons:
   – Competitors offer a better deal.
   – Problems seem too difficult to solve.
   – Personalities clash.
   – Negotiating styles clash.

Most negotiations will encounter difficult problems. There is a much greater chance that solutions will be found if both parties keep sight of the main objectives and maintain a positive tone.

3 Karen and Andrew put obstacles in the way. They continuously say no. They need to lift their eyes and keep the overall objective in mind. In this way, they could maintain a more positive tone.

4 Examples of both Andrew and Karen's negative responses:
'We cannot be expected to take on all your team ...'
'Beyond that we can't commit ourselves.'
'We cannot afford to offer contracts ...'

5 She makes sure the overall objective remains visible:
'Our main priority is to give a good quality, value for money service.'
She is very clear about what they can do and what they can't. She expresses their position clearly and positively.

6 She uses the concession to maintain a positive approach while ruling out taking on all their staff:
'We won't be able to do that. We might be able to take on one other person ...'

Language knowledge

1

Extract	concession	condition
one	one per cent reduction in monthly fee	guarantee on quantity (annual contract)
two	finance through customer	competitive rates (two per cent below base rate over five years)
three	sixty days payment terms	penalty for late payment (one per cent per day)
four	preferred supplier	turnover-related discount

2 **a** Extract one
   If you could offer us an annual contract, we would be happy to give you the one per cent.
   b Extract two
   We've got the contract if we come to you for the money.
   c Extract three
   If you were late paying, we would want an extra penalty payment.
   d Extract four
   If they came up with a better offer, we'd give you the chance to match it.

3 Here are some suggestions. Other responses are possible.
   a I'm afraid we'll have to cancel the contract unless you reduce your fees.
   b We'll have to choose another supplier if you can't make us a better offer.
   c That looks like the end of the negotiation, unless you can make a concession.
   d I'm afraid you'll lose your job unless you improve your performance.
   e If you can't offer me a better salary than that, I'll leave the company.
   f I'll accept the new job only if I get a bigger office.

4 Here are some suggestions. Other responses are possible.
   a We could offer you a two per cent discount if you guaranteed the orders.
   b We might consider a firm order if you could offer early delivery.
   c What would you say if we offered you a new car? On one condition, you reach your sales targets.
   d We might be able to offer you a position on the board if you agreed to work overseas.
   e We could organize a new office if you agreed to work this weekend.
   f We might consider a salary rise if you were prepared to move to Liverpool.

5 A: We seem to have reached a stalemate. We're not going to progress *unless* you can make us a better offer.
   B: We might be able to offer something better, but *on one condition*.
   A: What's that?
   B: You would have to guarantee us a fixed order every month for a year.
   A: We might be able to do that, *as long as* we feel you are the right supplier for us.
   B: OK. If you *could* give us this guarantee, we *would* be prepared to reduce our prices by fifteen per cent.

7 1 offer   5 exceed
   2 equals   6 amount
   3 estimated   7 bargaining
   4 defeat   8 surrender

8 a We asked the supplier to put in a new *bid*. They did, and it not only *matched* other offers we had received, it actually *beat* them.
   b I don't enjoy *haggling*. I always get knocked down on price and end up *conceding* to the seller.
   c Unfortunately, we lost the contract. One of the competitors *outbid* us by a considerable *margin*.
   d We *quoted* them what we believed was a fair price, but they are not happy. They are going to want to *bargain*.

Unit 8

Communication skills

1 It is important to round off a negotiation well, so that nothing remains ambiguous. Before closing the negotiation, the participants need to confirm what exactly has been achieved. They need to agree on future follow-up action and, if possible, set a date for the next or future meetings.

3 She should have summarized, identified future actions, clarified any outstanding points, and closed on a positive note.

4 Karen is angry because Andrew is no longer working as a team member. He is fed up with the negotiation and wants to leave as soon as possible. He feels if they stay any longer, they will concede more. She feels they need to resolve some outstanding issues.

5 Françoise handles the closing session well. She summarizes, clarifies, and plans the next steps. She ends on a positive note.

6 She summarizes: *So, we have agreed an initial one-year contract ...*
   She agrees action: *We will meet again here to interview ...*
   She apologizes for leaving quickly: *I'm afraid I have to go now. I'm sorry I have to leave so abruptly.*

7 Checklist for closing a negotiation.
   Summarizing
   – summarize issues discussed
   – confirm objectives attained
   – state areas where you have yet to reach agreement or where further discussion is needed

   Follow-up action
   – reiterate what the next steps are: what follow-up action is required?
   – delegate responsibilty for follow-up action and set time-scale
   – minute or document decisions

   Departing
   – confirm arrangements for next meeting (if there is to be one)
   – chairperson thanks participants for coming
   – part on a positive note

Language knowledge

1

Extract		one	two	three	four
a	Summary of points of agreement/disagreement	✓		✓	✓
b	Follow-up action e.g. minutes of the meeting, further contacts	✓	✓	✓	✓
c	positive ending	✓	✓	✓	✓

2

a Indicate the end of the meeting:
Extract one: *So, I think we can call it a day.*
Extract two: *Let's stop there.*

b Introduce a summary:
Extract one: *Now, can I just clarify the main areas of agreement and those that are still left open?*
Extract two: *I'd just like to clarify the delivery terms again.*
Extract three: *So, let me just run over that again.*
Extract four: *So, just before we finish, could we go over the main points of the agreement?*

c Talk about follow-up action:
Extract one: *Patrick, can you draft that and circulate it before the next meeting?*
We'll aim to let you have our ideas by the beginning of next week.
Extract two: *Right. I'll get the minutes typed up so we both know what's been agreed so far.*
Extract three: *Would you like it in writing?*
Extract four: *She'll let you have a detailed summary.*
I'll send you a copy of the project management system we use.

d End on a positive note:
Extract one: *Good. So, it only remains for me to thank you for coming over. It's been a very productive meeting.*
Extract two: *Fine. Well, thank you for coming over. I think we've made very good progress.*
Extract three: *Anyway, we look forward to another good year.*
Extract four: *So, that's a major step we've taken.*

3

a Let me just *run/go over* the main points.
b I think that just about *covers* it.
c It *remains for me to* say how much we appreciate your contribution.
d Does that accurately *reflect* what we agreed during the meeting?
e Could you *draft* a written proposal before the next meeting?
f I *suggest* we meet later in the week. Would that suit you?
g As *far as* payment *is concerned*, there are still some *outstanding* issues to resolve.
h I'm afraid we didn't *get as far* as we hoped.
i Let's *call it a* day.

4a

a fruitful　　b helpful　　c useful　　d informative　　e stimulating
f interesting

b Here are some suggestions. There are many other possible responses.

  a *Thank you very much for coming over today.*
   That was a really productive meeting.

  b *I hope you found the meeting worthwhile.*
   I think that was very fruitful.

  c *I am delighted we had a chance for this preliminary meeting.*
   I found it extremely helpful.

  d *It was good of you to give up your time today.*
   The meeting was really useful.

  e *I think we covered the most important points.*
   I think we all agree that was very informative.

  f *In terms of our objectives, I think we did a good job.*
   It was an extremely stimulating meeting!

5 A: So that *brings* us to the end of a very *fruitful* negotiation. It's been a pleasure to work with you today. Let me just *run over* the areas of agreement and also highlight one or two *outstanding* issues which we still need to *resolve*. Firstly, we have *agreed* a quota of 160,000 units per month. Secondly, we have *committed* ourselves to processing at least 150,000 every four weeks. Thirdly, and just as important, we will manage the stock much more actively. Is that an accurate *summary*?

  B: That's fine. I just wanted to *add* that we think the 160,000 is a conservative figure.

  A: You may well be right. Let's review it again in six months. There were two *issues* which have been *left* open. There's the question of rejects and how we handle them, and there is also the more difficult problem of payment. I *suggest* we meet again next week to try to *resolve* these issues. Would that be *OK*?

  B: Fine. Shall we *say* next Thursday at, um, ten o'clock?

  A: Fine. See you then.

Listening Tapescript

Unit 1
Exercises 1, 2, and 3

Extract one

A: On behalf of Unica, I am very glad to welcome you to our head office. Shall we just go round the table, making sure we all know each other? Peter, why don't you start?

B: Right. Hello, everyone. My name's Peter Snelson. I'm the Corporate Affairs Director here in the UK, and I'll be in charge of producing the press statements when we have finalized the terms of our agreement.

A: Thanks, Peter. Ulrike?

C: Yes, hello. I'm Ulrike Kristofferson, in charge of Strategic Marketing, and I'd just like to say how pleased I am that we have all finally got together. And that we are making a start on what I'm sure will be a vital alliance in our industry.

A: Thank you. Yves, would you like to introduce your team?

D: Of course. Well, I'm Yves Canaux, Group Marketing Director, Europe. This is Luca Gardini. He looks after our offices in Southern Europe.

E: Good morning. Nice to meet you all, at last.

D: And I think everyone knows Gabriella? (some sounds of agreement)

F: Yes, I think I spoke to everyone when I was setting up this meeting.

D: And finally, there's Dieter Weiss from our office in Ulm ...

Extract two

A: Giorgio, come in. Take a seat.

B: Thanks.

A: So, how are you? How are the family?

B: They're all fine, thanks. My youngest daughter has just gone off to university, actually. The other two left home last year, so now it's just my wife and me at home.

A: So do you miss them a lot, or are you just enjoying the peace and quiet?

B: A little bit of both. I've certainly had more time for work over the last year or so.

A: Yes, well, we had noticed. And that was actually one of the things I wanted to discuss with you this morning. So, shall we start by looking at your last appraisal?

B: Well, I wondered if I could start by saying how I see things at the moment?

A: Of course. Go ahead.

Extract three

A: Hi, Elena, good to see you again. How are you?

B: Fine thanks. And you?

A: I'm fine, apart from being in the middle of moving house, which is a nightmare. But I'll appreciate not having to spend so much time travelling to work every day!

B: Yes, it took me nearly two hours to get here this morning. The traffic was appalling.

A: I guess you could do with a coffee, then?

B: Thanks, that would be nice.

A: Milk, sugar?

B: Black, two sugars, please.

A: So, how's business in your sector?

B: Not too bad. We've got a lot of work to do for the new budgets at this time of year.

A: Would you say that it's been better than last year?

B: I think so, certainly in my unit, we've seen an upturn in sales.

Extract four

A: How was your weekend?

B: OK. We went for a great walk along the river on Sunday. The weather was fantastic. How about you?

A: I didn't get back from the States until Saturday night, and I spent Sunday recovering. I still feel pretty jet-lagged.

B: You must be exhausted! Perhaps you should have another coffee. It'll help you to stay awake!

C: OK, everyone, sorry to interrupt, but I think we'd better get started now. We've got a very full agenda. Has everybody met Sunita, our new PR Manager?

C: Well, Sunita, we're throwing you in at the deep end, I'm afraid. Now, the first thing we really need to do today is come up with some firm proposals ...

Exercise 5

a Well, I'm delighted to welcome you all to our processing plant here in Gdansk.

b Let me introduce you to Mehmet Tarkan. He's our key Account Manager.

c How was the weather when you left home?
d How was the flight over?
e Is everything OK with the hotel?
f Right, let's get started then.

Unit 2
Exercises 1 and 2
Extract one

A: So welcome back to what I hope will be our final session. On the agenda today we have just two items – the penalty clause, and payment terms. I suggest we aim to deal with the penalty issue before lunch – we've booked a table at the restaurant over the road for one o'clock. Then we can proceed with payment terms after lunch. Marc here is going to take the minutes, and José Mañuel Molina, our Head of Legal Affairs, is here to advise us if we need him. So, before we start, let me just summarize what we agreed at the last session.

Extract two

B: I think you all know each other, so let's get down to business straight away. I know two of you need to be away by four this afternoon to catch flights, so I suggest we start with pricing policy immediately. Mai Lin, I think you're going to give us a brief presentation?

Extract three

C: So, thank you for coming, everyone. It really is a pleasure to see you all here. Firstly, may I suggest we start by taking a look at the agenda I sent you? Are there any comments on this?

D: Yes. I wondered whether we could take the patent question first. We really need to agree about that before anything else.

C: That's true, but it's also a potentially difficult area. That's the reason why I put it last. I thought it might be a good idea for us to start by confirming the points we have in common. We'll move on to the patent issue after that.

D: OK, well, that seems reasonable.

C: Sure? Well, then, before we go any further, I'd just like to say how strongly I feel that it's in both our interests to reach an agreement today. The market's becoming ever more competitive and our combined strength will give us some big advantages. Not least in terms of the dealer network. Now, I think Cristina would like to say a few words about that ...

Extract four

E: So, as we all know, we're here today to try and reach agreement about a long-term delivery contract. Up to now, you've supplied us with some of our major components, but only on a monthly basis. What we're looking for is an annual contract for the supply of three key components. Now, as you know, we've read your offer and we've drawn up an agenda for today, which covers the main areas for negotiation – that is price, payment terms, and quality guarantees. Are you happy about all that?

F: Yes, that seems fine.

E: How are you fixed for time?

F: No problem. As long as it takes.

E: Fine. By the way, I hope you don't mind if Irina sits in? She's just joined the Purchasing Department and I'd like her to see how we manage a contract like this. Is that OK?

F: Of course. No problem.

E: So, let's have a look at your pricing proposals.

Extract five

A: OK now, we've got some difficult points here so I suggest we try and stick to a procedure. Firstly, we'll ask you to spell out the advantages of your offer, and then we'll have a question and answer session to resolve any outstanding issues. Anything we don't manage to clarify at this stage can then be tabled for discussion later. But we'll keep going through the contract, making sure at each stage that we all understand exactly what's on the table. Is that acceptable?

B: Yes, that's a good idea.

A: Christian has volunteered to keep note of the outstanding issues, and I hope by lunchtime we will have got through all the main clauses. We can always come back to any contentious clauses after lunch.

Extract six

C: So, let's get started right away. Marian, I believe you've got some proposals for this year's contract which you'd like us to hear?

D: That's right. We thought we could briefly run through the offer, and answer any questions you may have.

C: OK, fine. I've got another meeting at three this afternoon, so that gives us most of today, and we can meet up again tomorrow if we need to. So, over to you, Marian.

D: Thanks. Well, there are three main sections to the offer we would like you to ...

Unit 3
Exercises 1 and 2
Extract one

A: Now, what I'd like to do is tell you about our range of superb services. It's going to take about five minutes and I've got some slides to show you. I'm sure you are aware of our track record in this field, so I'm not going to be giving specific client references as I go through. That way we save on time. So, if you're ready, I'd like to start off by talking about our driving range support. You can't beat us on price or delivery in this area ...

Extract two

A: Right, since we're short of time I'd like to make this a question and answer session, but if you've got any comments, please feel free to interrupt. We'll try to answer any points as fully as we can. So, as I understand it, what you're looking for is a range of support services for the chain of golfing equipment outlets. Is that right?

B: Yes, that's right.

A: Well, I think the most appropriate thing is for me to run through what we've done for similar operations. You've seen our brochures, so I'll concentrate on a couple of specific examples, and then go into more detail. Does that sound useful?

B: Fine. Go ahead.

A: OK. So, as you can see here on the first slide, I've put the details of our most recent client ...?

Extract three

A: When our team tried to identify the main issues for our meeting today, we came up with three important areas: price, delivery, and quality guarantees. Would you agree that those are our main concerns?

B: Yes, those are certainly the key issues.

A: Fine, so I suggest we go through them separately, in order. We'll tell you our position with regard to each, and you can give us your response as we talk. Is that OK?

B: Fine.

A: Now, on the price question, I expect you've had time to see our proposals. I just wanted to add that these are standard prices and we are in a position to negotiate discounts for sizeable orders ...

Extract four

A: There are three main points I'd like to cover, starting with pricing. Now, as you can see on this slide, there's a very close relationship between price and quantity. Let me just take you through these figures.

B: Um ... could I just ask ...?

A: I'd prefer to take questions at the end, if you don't mind, OK? Now, as I was saying, there is a close relationship between prices and quantity. Starting in the first row, column one, you'll see quantities of up to a hundred at a fixed price of twenty-two pence a unit. Now, if we jump down to row five, we see quantities of ...

B: Sorry, I don't quite understand.

A: Just bear with me. We see quantities of over two hundred units ...

Unit 4
Exercises 1 and 2

Extract one

A: So, you can see that what we're offering is a total package. I'd just like to talk you through the different elements. (*pause*) Now, the core of the contract is, of course, the maintenance provision. We aim to supply a round-the-clock, fully operational team of maintenance engineers. (*pause*) They will be working under a supervisor who will be recruited from the existing team. (*pause*)

B: Look, sorry to digress, but what I'd particularly like to ask you about are the payment terms.

A: Oh, right, OK. Well, what exactly is it that you want to know?

C: Well, to start with, we think that there's a problem with this round-the-clock service.

A: Oh, and what's that?

B: Can we come back to that in a minute? What I still don't understand is how the system of invoicing us monthly is going to work out in practice.

A: Yes, of course. Can we have a look at that now ...?

Extract two

A: So what we're offering is a total package. I'd like to talk you through the different elements, if that's OK?

B: Fine, go ahead

A: Now the core of the contract is the maintenance provision. We aim to supply a round-the-clock, fully operational team of maintenance engineers. (*pause*)

C: May I ask a question?

A: Of course.

C: What exactly do you mean by 'fully operational'?

A: Well, these engineers will be trained and equipped to deal with both standard and emergency maintenance work. We would expect them to be able to handle anything from a faulty valve to, for example, a total shut-down. This means that if the machines ever break down, whatever the scale of the problem, there is always someone on hand to deal with it immediately. Is that all clear?

C: Yes, thanks.

A: So, shall I go on?

B: Please do.

A: This team will work to a supervisor who will be recruited from the existing maintenance staff. Now ...

B: Just a minute, Alex. Could you clarify something for me? As you know, we're looking for a new approach, which is much tighter, more dynamic. Aren't we going to run into problems with ...

Extract three

B: I think you've overestimated the need for night supervision. Your costs for that look very high to me.

A: Well, perhaps I should explain how we got to those figures? (*pause*) What we did was to calculate on a three-shift basis, with the night shift – that's ten till six – using just a skeleton staff. Now, at the moment, you run just one line ...

B: OK. But hang on a moment. What I still don't understand is your idea of 'skeleton staff'.

A: What do you mean? The number of people?

B: Well, yes. How on earth can you justify three engineers working through the night?

A: I'm just coming to that.

C: And there's another thing. Your prices for management control look rather high.

A: Ah, well, there, you see, it's a question of quality ...

Extract four

A: I was just going to explain how we have planned the staffing ratios, if that's OK?

B: Fine. Go ahead.

A: We've looked at your current ratios. We think they're higher than they need to be.

B: Yes, I think you might well be right there.

A: So we then looked at the industry average for maintenance staff levels, and we came up with a ratio of one engineer to every hundred units of production.

B: That's interesting. It means that in our sector we currently have about double the industry average.

A: That's right. We're suggesting that you reduce your current figure initially by twenty-five per cent. So most of the maintenance shifts would go down from four to three engineers.

C: Wouldn't it be better to come into line with the industry average and cut it to two?

A: That's what I'd like to aim for in the second year. We feel it's too big a reduction to make immediately.

Exercise 3

a I think one of the critical questions is staff levels.

b There are two things we need to look at: firstly, maintenance, and secondly, safety.

c As you know, we have considerable experience in your field.

d We have concentrated over the last few months on improving standards.

e Our biggest challenge in the coming year will be coping with the new environmental legislation, and the effect this will have on our production processes.

Exercise 4

a Our sales have responded to the changes in market conditions, and we reached a high point this month.

b We've got the best person for the job, so we don't have to look any further.

c We've sent out a lot of invitations, so we expect large numbers to attend.

d The costs have come down, so we are able to offer much more competitive prices.

e We have already spent much too long on this project.

Exercise 6

a Would you like to hear about the cost breakdown?

b Shall we take a break for lunch?

c I've told you about the technical side of things. Shall I outline the commercial package we are offering?

d I'll start by pointing out the pluses and minuses of the joint venture. Does that sound OK?

e And when you're ready, I'll just finish with a brief summary of our development plans for next year.

Unit 5
Exercises 1 and 2

Extract one

A: I'm afraid we're all going to have to accept cuts in our budgets. There's no way of avoiding it.

B: Well, you can cut my budget if you want. Just don't expect the sort of sales I've predicted, that's all I'm saying.

A: Charles, we're trying to make this decision in as constructive a way as possible.

B: I'm not being destructive. I'm just saying if you touch my budget, sales will go down. If that's what you want, fair enough. I agree to a cut in my budget.

Extract two

A: What about you, Marta?

C: Well, I can see we need to share the cuts across the company, but we also have to decide what is essential and what is more peripheral.

B: Well, I can't see what's more essential to the company than sales.

A: Just a moment, Charles. Let's hear what Marta has to say.

B: What she said is that we have to decide what's essential and what isn't. And it's completely obvious that a cut in her training budget is less damaging than a cut in my sales budget.

C: I'm sorry, but I don't see it that way. I've got a relatively small budget, but it's a key element in the development plan.

B: Sure, sure, but some of the training you organize is hardly central. I mean, assertiveness training – what's that all about?

Extract three

A: OK, Marta, let's come back to your budget.

C: Before we make a decision, I'd just like to emphasize that training has been central to the positive changes we've made in the last couple of years.

A: Yes, you're right of course. But I think we'd all agree that a delay in some of the training programmes wouldn't necessarily be too critical to the business.

C: There may be one or two programmes we could put back, but I'm not sure ...

Extract four

A: Dan, I'm afraid it's your turn. I'd like to look at the IT budget. Now, I know we've had a lot of investment over the last few years in this area.

D: That's true, but it's very much part of a long-term plan. The upgrading of the system was started three years ago, and we're about sixty per cent of the way through. In my opinion, it would be disastrous to call a halt at this stage.

A: Nobody is suggesting we should call a halt. It's more a question of rescheduling.

Language focus

1 Your prices are a bit high. (*single pitch, serious*)
   Your prices are a bit high. (*rising intonation, positive tone*)

2 Wouldn't you agree? (*falling tone, threatening*)
   Wouldn't you agree? (*rising tone, encouraging*)

Exercise 5

Version 1

(Falling or flat intonation – discouraging tone.)

A: I'm afraid your figures for last year don't look so good.
B: No, they could be better.
A: I'm not sure how we can do business on this basis.
B: Sorry, could you explain?
A: Well, we're worried about your track record. It could be stronger.
B: I'm surprised you should say that. Perhaps you've forgotten some of our excellent customer references?
A: No, I haven't forgotten. It's just that they haven't been with you for very long.
B: I think you'll find that we have some very well-established clients. For example, we've been working with Phoenix International for five years.
A: I'm afraid we like to see a slightly longer track record.
B: I understand, but as I'm sure you know, we've only been in business for six years!

Version 2

(Repeat of previous dialogue but with rising intonation, higher pitch – positive tone.)

Unit 6

Exercises 1 and 2

A: I would like to suggest we seriously consider Andreas. He's very experienced and I like his attitude.
B: I'm surprised, Maura. I thought you would go for Francesca, having already worked with her.
A: I'm sure Francesca would do a good job. It's more a question of priorities. I'd like to keep her on the KL project next year. Who do you propose, then, Nigel?
B: I think we should go for Francesca. OK, she's very busy at the moment. But I think this new project is going to be very tough and she has the right background.
C: What about Peter McVitie? He's an obvious candidate, surely? He's pretty free at the moment, he speaks the language, and he's a very good team leader.
A: That's all true, Ute, but don't you think it's time we gave Andreas a chance?
C: His time will come. I really strongly advise you to go for Peter. It's vital we have the right person for such an important job.

Exercise 3

a Why don't we take a break now?
b I propose we wait until Christmas.
c I advise you to hire this woman.
d I would propose that we delay the decision.
e I think we should hire the man.
f I want us to cancel the project.

Unit 7

Exercises 1 and 2

Extract one

A: Look, we're going round and round in circles here. What we need is some sort of concession.
B: Well, we could offer you a slight reduction in the monthly fee – on certain conditions, obviously.
A: OK, what do you have in mind?
B: Well, possibly up to one per cent, but we would need a guarantee on quantity.
A: What sort of guarantee?
B: Well, if you could offer us an annual contract rather than just month-by-month orders, I think we would be happy to give you the one per cent.

Extract two

A: Unless you are prepared to offer some kind of incentive, I think we might as well call it a day.
B: What sort of incentive do you have in mind?
A: Well, if you win this contract, you're going to need a lot of capital up front. We've got our own venture capital business. We'd like you to come to us for the financing.
B: So, effectively, what you're saying is, we've got the contract if we come to you for the money? (*Yes.*) One condition: we'd need a very competitive offer on terms.
A: What do you have in mind?
B: Well, perhaps two per cent below base rate over five years.

Extract three

A: What would you say if we offered to be more flexible over payment? I'm thinking of sixty days instead of thirty.
B: That sounds interesting. Would there be any conditions?
A: Well, we'd be happy to agree to sixty days so long as that was the maximum. If you were late paying, we would want an extra penalty payment.
B: What sort of penalty are we talking about?
A: Well, I think it would have to be related to how many days you were late. Probably an additional one per cent for each day's delay.

Extract four

A: What could you offer us if we made you our preferred supplier?
B: I'm not sure I understand what you mean.
A: Well, we would give you the first opportunity to quote for any new business.
B: I see what you mean, but how would that actually work?

A: Well, we would ask you for a quote. If we were happy with the price you were asking, you'd get the contract. If we weren't satisfied, we'd ask another supplier for a quote. If they came up with a better offer, we'd give you a chance to match it.

B: Right. Well, on those terms we might be able to offer you a turnover-related discount. We could come up with a scale which reduced the monthly invoice depending on the overall turnover.

Unit 8
Exercises 1 and 2
Extract one

A: So, I think we can call it a day. Unfortunately, we didn't get as far as we would have liked to, but we've taken a step in the right direction. Now, can I just run over the main areas of agreement and those that are still left open? Firstly, we've agreed to limit the territory to the UK and France. That means that either side can negotiate other licence deals outside these countries. However, we've committed ourselves to informing each other of any further licence agreements. Is that right?

B: Yes, although I'd just like to add that the terms of any subsequent licence deal are entirely up to the licensing party.

A: Of course. Now the other item we were able to agree on was royalty fees and we have written those down for inclusion in a draft contract. Patrick, can you draft that and circulate it before the next meeting?

C: Certainly.

A: Now, that leaves two outstanding issues: firstly, payment terms, and secondly, a penalty clause. I suggest we go away and put together a written proposal on these. We'll aim to let you have our ideas by the beginning of next week. Is that acceptable?

B: Absolutely. I think that would be very helpful.

A: Good. So it only remains for me to thank you for coming over. It's been a very productive meeting. We'll look forward to seeing you here again on the fourteenth, and let's hope we can reach agreement on everything else.

Extract two

A: Let's stop there. It's getting late, and I've got an early meeting in the morning. Could you manage tomorrow afternoon?

B: Umm ... yes, later on. Say, four o'clock?

A: Right. I'll get the minutes typed up so we both know what's been agreed so far. Is there anything you want to add?

B: I'd just like to clarify the delivery terms again.

A: Could we leave that until tomorrow afternoon?

B: OK. Let's do that.

A: Fine. Well, thank you for coming over. I think we've made very good progress. I'll see you tomorrow at four.

Extract three

A: So, let me just run over that again. We've agreed a two per cent cut on the main product line next year, with a slight increase – just one per cent – on the two other lines. We expect delivery times to be as before and payment will be tightened up – not later than thirty days in future. Well, I think that just about covers it. Would you like it in writing?

B: Yes, if that's OK. I think you've got a very good deal there.

A: I would have liked more, but you've been a very reliable supplier for a long time, and we've all got to make a living, haven't we?

B: It's getting harder and harder. Anyway, we look forward to another good year.

Extract four

A: So, just before we finish, could we go over the main points of the agreement?

B: Certainly. We've reached agreement on the three main issues – that is personnel, finance, and marketing. On the personnel front, we have agreed to provide three project members each. For finance, we've agreed to publish monthly accounts and to use an external auditor to go through the figures on a six-monthly basis. Now, as far as marketing is concerned, we've agreed to combine our efforts, especially in this first important phase. Does that reflect at all what we said?

A: Yes, it does. I just wanted to add that we hope to have a detailed marketing plan ready by the end of the month, and that would then be an opportunity to see how we can best pool our resources.

B: Good. That sounds great. So, Anna has been keeping copious notes. She'll let you have a detailed summary. Now, we still need to look at the project management side, so I suggest we meet again. How about this time next week?

A: Just a moment ... Yes, that looks fine. In the meantime, I'll send you a copy of the project management system we use. Perhaps you can have a look at it before the next meeting.

B: I certainly will. So, that's a major step we've taken. Let's hope the project itself goes well!

A: I'm sure it will.

Exercise 4b

a Thank you very much for coming over today.

b I hope you found the meeting worthwhile.

c I'm delighted we had a chance for this preliminary meeting.

d It was good of you to give up your time today.

e I think we covered the most important points.

f In terms of our objectives, I think we did a good job.

Video Transcript

Unit 1 Preparing the ground
Version 1

ANDREW: You sure you don't want one, Karen?

KAREN: Not for me.

ANDREW: Of course, I don't know Françoise at all, but you've got to be on your guard with Sean. I told you about negotiating with him in Dallas two years ago, didn't I?

KAREN: I'm sure you did, Andrew. Can we just focus on the final package? We mustn't get stuck on the price. They're going to want to knock us down, but we have got some room to manoeuvre.

ANDREW: That's right. Sean was Head of Procurement at TEC in Atlanta.

KAREN: What we must keep in mind is a fall-back position if they push us on staff cuts.

ANDREW: Oh, we don't need to worry about that, Karen. We'll just play it by ear. Sean, how are you?

SEAN: Good to see you again, Andrew. Atlanta, wasn't it?

ANDREW: Dallas, actually.

SEAN: Right, three years ago.

ANDREW: Two.

SEAN: Yeah. Sure. You two know each other, right?

FRANÇOISE: You must be Karen Black. I'm Françoise Quantin. Welcome to Levien.

KAREN: We've spoken on the phone, haven't we? This is Andrew Carter, our Export Sales Executive.

ANDREW: Sorry, I thought you two already knew each other.

SEAN: Well, we all know each other now. Can we ...?

FRANÇOISE: Before we start, would you like a coffee?

KAREN: That would be nice.

FRANÇOISE: Milk?

KAREN: Yes, please.

Version 2

ANDREW: There you go.

KAREN: Thanks.

ANDREW: So, we'll wait for them to respond to our proposal.

KAREN: Yes, we know that the staff cuts and the price are the main issues, but we'd better let them set the agenda.

ANDREW: And you'd still like me to do the presentation?

KAREN: That's what we head-hunted you for, Andrew.

ANDREW: And you'll watch for their reactions and ...

KAREN: And deal with any questions. Yes.

ANDREW: Be careful with Sean, Karen. He drives a hard bargain.

KAREN: I'm sure I can handle him. We're in for a long day, aren't we?

ANDREW: Well, you did pack a toothbrush, didn't you?

FRANÇOISE: Sorry to have kept you waiting. You must be Karen Black. I'm Françoise Quantin and this is Sean Morrissey.

SEAN: Good to meet you, Karen. Françoise, this is my old sparring partner, Andrew Carter.

FRANÇOISE: Nice to meet you, Andrew. How was your flight?

KAREN: Excellent. Less than an hour.

ANDREW: Hardly time for the breakfast they serve.

FRANÇOISE: What about a coffee then, before we start?

SEAN: Yeah, you can bring it through.

FRANÇOISE: There's no need to hurry. Karen?

SEAN: Andrew, you'll have another one?

ANDREW: Please. Milk, three sugars.

FRANÇOISE: Sit down, please.

ANDREW: Are you missing the States, Sean?

SEAN: Yeah, I'm missing the kids and my wife. Andrew and I negotiated a deal in Dallas two years ago.

ANDREW: Yes, quite a marathon – thirty-six hours, wasn't it?

SEAN: Andrew, if a job's worth doing, it's worth doing well.

FRANÇOISE: Perhaps we had better start now.

Unit 2 Setting the agenda
Version 1

FRANÇOISE: We have studied your proposal with interest and, generally it seems to fit with our needs. But I am especially worried about cuts to my team.

KAREN: Perhaps Andrew could present our proposal and then you'll see …

FRANÇOISE: I'm sure you can understand my concern. I have a team of four people in IT. They are very dedicated, of course, but they are very unsettled.

ANDREW: Can I suggest we present the pluses for you if you choose Okus, then perhaps we can identify your areas of …

SEAN: We do need some assurances here. Any cuts are going to need approval from the Works Council.

FRANÇOISE: We must sort this out before we continue.

KAREN: I see. Have you got the documents about rehiring staff? As I'm sure you'll understand, staffing is a major cost area for us and the prices are based on the staffing proposal we've made. Now, if you can agree to the prices before we go on …

SEAN: No, we can talk prices later. We want to resolve the staffing issues first. They're two separate problems.

ANDREW: But what Karen is saying is that the two are dependent.

SEAN: Not for us they're not. We want closure on the staffing issue first. Yours isn't the only offer on the table you know.

Version 2

FRANÇOISE: I'd like to start by saying a few words about the meeting today and what we expect to achieve. One thing I'd like to clarify from the start is that we see Okus as a strong candidate, but, of course, not the only one. What we hope to do today is to find enough common ground. Is that clear?

KAREN: Fine.

FRANÇOISE: I've drawn up an agenda. First we'd like you to present your proposal. We have read it, but we'd like you to go over the critical areas. Andrew, I understand you've come prepared to do this?

ANDREW: It should take about ten, fifteen minutes. Please feel free to ask any questions while I'm talking.

FRANÇOISE: Good. That will help us to identify issues which need more discussion. After that I suggest we try and resolve any outstanding differences and then, finally, assuming that we can agree, I thought we could draw up an action plan for the next few months.

SEAN: I just want to add that you can use the room next door anytime. There's coffee and stuff there if you need it.

KAREN: Thanks.

FRANÇOISE: What about the end of the day? Are you flying back this evening?

KAREN: Yes, well, we could get rooms at one of the airport hotels.

SEAN: I'm sure we can get you somewhere better than that.

FRANÇOISE: Hopefully, you won't need a hotel.

Unit 3 Establishing positions
Version 1

ANDREW: And as you can see, we also have a broad range of clients in various industries. For example, we recently took over IT management at Central …

FRANÇOISE: We know all this, Andrew. It's the offer you've made us that we're interested in.

ANDREW: Of course, yes. Let me … Here we are. We've broken this down by department …

SEAN: Sorry.

KAREN: Andrew, sorry to interrupt, but perhaps Françoise and Sean would like to hear about control systems, pricing, and staffing levels.

SEAN: Staffing would be good.

ANDREW: Yes. Sorry. Yes, I'm sure I've got another overhead on that. We've looked at your – here we are – at your current levels of IT operation and support …

SEAN: That's great, Andrew, but what I really want to know is – are you going to hire our staff or not?

KAREN: Andrew, perhaps I should answer that. As you know, staffing levels depend on the level of service you decide to go for. The one you choose depends on the degree of service and support you require.

Version 2

ANDREW: So, moving on, I'd like to focus quickly on the three critical areas, and then hear your response. Now, this slide covers management control. As this is really the make or break factor in an outsourcing contract, we've really got to match, and then improve on, your own management systems. So, what we propose to do is put one permanent manager on site and one support engineer as well. Any questions so far?

SEAN: And who'd deal with special projects or problems?

ANDREW: Our plan for that would be to use our own UK-based engineers on an ad hoc basis.

FRANÇOISE: I'm not sure I understand how your project management system operates for urgent work.

ANDREW: We've used a similar approach on other contracts: the IT manager here would have day-to-day control, but when he or she needs help, that can be called in from Okus in the UK. Do you have any questions on this?

SEAN: But won't this be a first for you – servicing a contract overseas?

KAREN: Yes, that's right, but we do have similar clients in Edinburgh, for example, and time and distance wise, there's not a lot of difference between Belgium and Scotland. So we don't anticipate any problems on that score.

ANDREW: Perhaps you'd like to talk to our clients in Edinburgh?

FRANÇOISE: No. We have already followed up your references. Please go on.

ANDREW: Fine. Can I go on and talk a little bit about pricing?

Unit 4 Clarifying positions
Version 1

KAREN: No, what we're saying is that costs are based on a number of factors, the time of day, of course, is one of them. We keep a log of all call-outs and, if the figure for a month exceeds the fixed invoice fee, there'll be an adjustment the following month.

FRANÇOISE: What is the fixed invoice fee?

KAREN: The rates are on page twenty-two of the proposal. It depends ...

SEAN: What about the call-out rate?

KAREN: It depends on the time of day.

SEAN: Can you give me a ballpark figure?

FRANÇOISE: Where are the figures for project manager fees?

KAREN: Right. Andrew, have you got the rates for that? The point we'd like to stress is that we have calculated a global price, and you only pay more if you go over the generous level of support we have offered.

SEAN: Yeah, but do we get a choice on this?

KAREN: That was what I was saying. We have offered two levels of support. The basic level buys you ...

FRANÇOISE: Sorry, Karen, before you go on, I see Andrew has my figures for project management.

ANDREW: Our project manager rate is hourly, but if you look at the overall package, the rate can come out much lower than those figures.

SEAN: What about my options?

KAREN: They're spelt out on page thirty-four.

Version 2

KAREN: If you look at page twenty-two: what we do is keep a log of all call-outs and, if the figure for a month is more than the fixed invoice fee, we make an adjustment the following month.

FRANÇOISE: So, we can't be certain about how much the monthly invoice will be.

KAREN: It depends which level of support you opt for.

FRANÇOISE: Can you explain that?

KAREN: Certainly. As you can see, there are two levels. Level A is all inclusive. You pay a set fee, you specify what IT projects you want doing, and you don't pay anything extra.

FRANÇOISE: So our contract would specify all IT projects for the next five years.

KAREN: No, it's shorter term. We'd draw up an annual schedule.

SEAN: Okay. What's the difference between project and regular support work?

KAREN: Can I come back to that in a moment, Sean? I'd just like to get the two options out of the way. With Level A, you only pay a monthly bill. With Level B, there are no project management fees in the charge, so there would be additions to the monthly bill.

FRANÇOISE: So what we have to decide is how we want to pay: an even cost each month, or project by project.

KAREN: Which is Level B. Exactly.

SEAN: I still don't get it, Karen. When is it a project and when is it just regular support work?

ANDREW: As Karen was saying, we'd specify the projects in Level A. With Level B, the IT manager will need to get approval for each project as it comes up.

SEAN: Okay. Can we go over the approval process?

ANDREW: Yes. If you look at section three of the proposal, you'll see ...

Unit 5 Managing conflict
Version 1

ANDREW: We'll draw up a schedule of projects, which we both feel need to be carried out over the following year. These could be introducing new software, training, hardware upgrades ...

SEAN: Yeah, but how do we know when your guys are doing support work and when they're doing project work?

ANDREW: I think we will all know what type of work ...

SEAN: I don't think so. It will be in your guys' interest to log support work as project work and charge us for it at the month end.

ANDREW: Sean, I'm interested in a partnership – based on trust.

SEAN: Great ideal, Andrew, but you won't be on site working here, will you?

ANDREW: Me personally, no. I don't see your point.

SEAN: My point is that we won't know what your guys are doing.

ANDREW: But we're going to appoint a manager from your staff.

SEAN: Look Andrew, I've seen hundreds of these projects, and there's always room for manoeuvre. You haven't got a whole lot of experience in this type of contract.

ANDREW: Sean, I've been in this industry for fifteen years. I really don't see how you can call me inexperienced.

KAREN: Andrew, I don't think Sean was saying that. Can I suggest we take a break.

FRANÇOISE: Yes. A good idea. Why don't you go next door? There is coffee if you need it.

SEAN: Coffee'll be the last thing he'll need.

FRANÇOISE: What are you trying to do, Sean?

SEAN: What am I trying to do? I was just getting them right where I wanted them when you let them call a time-out.

FRANÇOISE: No. I will have to work with these people and I want a positive relationship. I don't see what we achieve by getting personal.

SEAN: It's tactics, Françoise. They were getting too comfortable there. It was time to shake them up.

FRANÇOISE: That may be the way you do things, but it's not the way I run things in my department.

Version 2

ANDREW: So we'll draw up a schedule of projects, which we both feel need to be carried out over the following year. These could be introducing new software, training, hardware upgrades …

SEAN: Sorry to interrupt, Andrew, but I still need to know when your guys are doing support work and when they're doing project work.

ANDREW: That does need to be clarified.

KAREN: What if we put something in the contract?

SEAN: That'd be a start. It's more the logging I worry about. You know if one of your guys has spent a couple of hours sorting out a problem with one of the PCs and then an hour back on our customer databases, won't he just think: 'Well, that's three hours of project work'?

ANDREW: I hope not, Sean. Our team will be working to your budget.

SEAN: I know that, Andrew, but who's going to supervise all this?

ANDREW: We have talked about taking on one of your team as our IT manager.

SEAN: Yeah. But you're still gonna bill us from the UK. It'll all be down to your log.

ANDREW: So it's the accuracy of the log that's worrying you?

SEAN: Yeah, that and the lack of experience here. Please, don't get me wrong. It's the people on the ground I'm worried about. We all know there can be a lot of room for manoeuvre with these contracts.

KAREN: I think I see what you're getting at, Sean. Can I suggest a break? Andrew and I need to talk this through a bit more.

FRANÇOISE: Good idea. Please use the room next door. How do you think it's going?

SEAN: OK. This logging business could be a nightmare though. We've got to find some way to make them drop it.

FRANÇOISE: Their Level A option does that.

SEAN: Yeah, but the cost of it. It'd be great if we could push them towards a global price for support and minimum project work.

FRANÇOISE: Could we suggest it?

SEAN: No. Let's see what they come up with.

Unit 6 Making and responding to proposals
Version 1

SEAN: So, what have you got for us?

KAREN: We'd like to make a proposal.

SEAN: Before you do that, let me explain our position.

KAREN: Go on.

SEAN: We don't like the concept of logging. We think that every call will be logged as project work and we could end up throwing money away. We want a global price to include support work and project work.

ANDREW: But that's exactly what our Level A package offers you.

SEAN: Your Level A package is prohibitive on cost.

KAREN: What?

SEAN: Expensive. We don't want to pay for something we don't use.

KAREN: We do understand that, Sean. That's why we feel we could offer you something between the two.

SEAN: We want a full support package with agreed IT projects for a fixed price. Okay? We don't want any suprises.

ANDREW: That's why we offered you Level A, Sean.

SEAN: And it's way too expensive, Andrew.

ANDREW: You can't have it both ways. You're asking for a Rolls Royce, but you're only willing to pay for a Ford. If you want complete security, you've got to pay for it.

SEAN: If you can't make it work, I guess we'll just have to look elsewhere.

Version 2

KAREN: We've discussed this problem of logging support and project work, and we'd like to make a proposal.

SEAN: Let's hear it.

KAREN: Firstly, we do understand your concerns about the pricing systems. Level A is too expensive and Level B holds too many potential surprises. So, we propose a level of support between A and B. We include all maintenance and support work at a fixed price, plus a minimum project load. How does that sound?

SEAN: Good, in theory. But I can't see any difference between that and Level A. We want to agree a monthly rate for essential support and project work.

KAREN: What about urgent, additional work?

FRANÇOISE: You could quote for that when it's necessary.

ANDREW: Wouldn't that be difficult to manage in reality? We could get delays while we waited for your approval.

KAREN: How would it work, Françoise?

FRANÇOISE: Maybe we could agree a contingency sum at the start of the year to cover urgent projects.

KAREN: Would the IT Manager have control of that?

FRANÇOISE: No, but I'm sure I could approve most of the work myself.

KAREN: At the risk of sounding excited, that could work.

ANDREW: Let's go back to the original proposal and put some figures to this.

SEAN: Great. Let's get started.

Unit 7 Bargaining
Version 1

FRANÇOISE: I'm very concerned about my team. I have to protect as many of these jobs as possible.

ANDREW: We understand your concerns, but we cannot be expected to take on all your team, and provide the cost-effective support you're looking for.

SEAN: I find that hard to believe, Andrew. With the support package we just negotiated you're gonna need people to service the contract.

KAREN: As we said, we plan to hire one of your existing IT team as project leader and one as a support engineer. Beyond that, we can't commit ourselves.

SEAN: We're not asking you to hire people for the rest of their lives, but we have to have more than two jobs to take back to the Works Council.

FRANÇOISE: This is very important to us, Karen. We can't sign this contract without commitment on this.

ANDREW: We cannot afford to offer contracts to all your staff on top of the support deal we've come up with. We've got our own team, and we're going to have to utilize them.

SEAN: Isn't that going to cost you a lot – sending them over here?

KAREN: We're losing sight of the objective here. We want to ...

FRANÇOISE: I am sorry, Karen, but we have to have commitment from you on staff.

KAREN: I see. Can I suggest another break then? Andrew and I need to discuss this.

FRANÇOISE: Please. Take your time.

ANDREW: We might as well call it a day.

KAREN: No, I haven't come all this way to get nothing.

ANDREW: Come on, Karen. They've driven us down over the support pricing and now they're asking for staffing commitments we can't make. We'd be crazy to sign up four members of Levien staff.

KAREN: What if we took on one more member of their team – on a one year contract – to work at Levien, but also at some of our other projects?

Version 2

FRANÇOISE: Can we return to the staffing question for a moment? As we said at the start, we have certain obligations to our four IT people.

KAREN: We do understand that. Our main priority is to give a good quality, value for money service. So, we think one of your team should become our project leader.

SEAN: OK.

KAREN: And another should become the support engineer.

FRANÇOISE: That's good, but we had hoped to safeguard all four jobs.

SEAN: We appreciate your flexibility on the support contract, Karen, but staffing is just as important. Labour laws here are real tough, and we probably won't be able to sign this contract if we don't get a better offer.

ANDREW: What are you looking for?

FRANÇOISE: I'd like to go back to the Works Council and tell them we can find work for all four members of my team.

SEAN: What about taking the other two on short-term contracts?

KAREN: We won't be able to do that. We might be able to take on one other person as a project engineer, but he ...

ANDREW: Or she ...

KAREN: Thank you, Andrew. They would have to be flexible about where they worked.

FRANÇOISE: But what about staff to cover this contract?

KAREN: We feel we can't guarantee more than the two jobs. We have our own project engineers to support the team here in Brussels.

SEAN: So, what's on the table for this third person? A one year contract based in Brussels?

ANDREW: Yes, but whoever does it would have to be prepared to work elsewhere as well.

FRANÇOISE: Three out of four. That would be something.

KAREN: Françoise, can we break for a few minutes? Andrew and I need to talk this through.

FRANÇOISE: Of course. Take your time.

KAREN: I think we're almost there.

ANDREW: Absolutely. We can go for a deal now.

KAREN: I do want them to understand that we select the staff we need.

ANDREW: Absolutely.

Unit 8 Conclusion and agreement
Version 1

FRANÇOISE: ... And you have agreed to take on all four members of our existing IT Department. We have confirmed the appointment of Bernard Lagisquet as your on-site IT manager.

KAREN: Wait a minute, Françoise. This isn't confirmed. We want to see if he's the right person.

FRANÇOISE: He is the best candidate.

SEAN: He's the only candidate.

KAREN: And he'll be an Okus employee, so we'd like to interview him.

FRANÇOISE: OK. Yes. A contingency sum will be agreed at the beginning of the year for urgent IT projects and I will be responsible for authorizing any spending.

KAREN: Will this be in the contract?

SEAN: No. I guess that about does it. It's been a very productive day – a definite result.

FRANÇOISE: I'm very pleased we managed to solve my staff problems. I don't think there's anything more ...

KAREN: I think there are a couple of things: a system for payment and employment contracts.

SEAN: You and Françoise can do that by phone. How about we order you a taxi?

KAREN: Could we just ...?

ANDREW: Thanks, Sean. If we go fairly soon, we can get the earlier flight.

KAREN: What are you doing? There's no way we're finished here.

ANDREW: Come on, Karen, let's just cut our losses and go home while we've still got something.

SEAN: You should make that dinner. Ten minutes.

ANDREW: Excellent.

FRANÇOISE: I'm afraid I have to go. Andrew, a pleasure to meet you.

ANDREW: Likewise.

KAREN: Françoise, I really think …

FRANÇOISE: Karen, I will call you tomorrow. I think we have made excellent progress today.

SEAN: We should be going too.

ANDREW: Yes, let's go. Karen?

KAREN: Yes, we can't do any more here, can we?

Version 2

FRANÇOISE: … And you have agreed to take on three of our existing IT Department: two permanently, and one on a short-term contract. Is that correct?

KAREN: Yes. We do understand you feel that Bernard is front runner for the job of IT manager. We would like to arrange an interview with him, though. Can we do that on the twentieth?

FRANÇOISE: That wouldn't be a problem. He will be working for you after all.

KAREN: Good.

ANDREW: Can we just clarify this contingency sum for urgent projects?

FRANÇOISE: Yes. Karen and I will agree a sum before the contract starts. I will sign for any expenditure.

ANDREW: Will it be the contract?

SEAN: The actual sum won't be.

ANDREW: I see.

SEAN: Let's put a clause in which details the contingency option without saying how much it'll be. We don't want any delays while we sort out the actual amount.

FRANÇOISE: We do want this to be up and running by the start of next year.

ANDREW: That sounds good.

FRANÇOISE: So, we have agreed an initial one-year contract on the basis of full support and minimal project work. We will meet again here to interview Bernard and you will fax us your standard employment contract for the two permanent staff. Can we leave it here for today?

KAREN: Could we discuss payment terms?

FRANÇOISE: Can we delay that until the next meeting? I'm afraid I have to go now.

SEAN: Fax us a proposed schedule and we can talk it through in two weeks.

KAREN: That'll be fine.

FRANÇOISE: I'm sorry I have to leave so abruptly. Sean will arrange a taxi for you.

KAREN: Thank you. See you in two weeks.

FRANÇOISE: Yes, you must stay the night and see more of Brussels.

ANDREW: That'd be great.

FRANÇOISE: Goodbye then. I hope we both got the deal we wanted.

KAREN: I think we did. Goodbye.